Antiquarian Books:
An Insider's Account

Antiquarian Books:
An Insider's Account

Roy Harley Lewis

ARCO PUBLISHING COMPANY, INC.

New York

Published by Arco Publishing Company, Inc.
219 Park Avenue South, New York, N.Y. 10003

Copyright © 1978 by Roy Harley Lewis

Library of Congress Cataloging in Publication Data

Lewis, Roy Harley.
    Antiquarian books.

    Bibliography: p. 193
    Includes index.
    1. Antiquarian booksellers. I. Title.
Z286. A55L48   658.8'09'070573   78-578
ISBN 0-668-04587-6

Contents

	Preface	*page* 7
1	Booksellers and Collectors	9
2	'Generous Liberal-Minded Men'	30
3	The Literary Detective	56
4	Anecdotes from the Book World	79
5	The Common Enemy: The Book Thief	95
6	The Detective at Bay	112
7	Sale by Auction	129
8	'Talismans and Spells'	155
9	Trends	182
	Selected Bibliography	193
	Index	195

Preface

The rôle played by antiquarian books in world trade is, financially, quite insignificant. Hundreds of medium-sized companies have a turnover greater than the whole of the antiquarian book and manuscript trade together. So what is it that attracts people into the business? Perhaps it is that the story behind those books and manuscripts has all the mystery and fascination of the message in the bottle at the mercy of the ocean currents: from where and in what circumstances did the books begin their journey?; through whose hands have they passed over the years, or even centuries?; where, if ever, will they finally come to rest? Perhaps is it also that in no other business, particularly in one of such importance and stature, could one find such a constantly rising sales graph, built entirely on the same recycled products.

The antiquarian-book trade is structured like an iceberg, with a great mass of booksellers—many operating from home and by post—forming the vast underwater base, and the select few forming the tip. Yet the activities of these few probably provide seventy per cent of the turnover. An élite group of individuals and companies, with different backgrounds, philosophies and selling patterns, their contribution to society makes them worthy of close study. One might ask why the bookseller should be any more interesting than the shoe salesman. Yet there can be few other careers that offer such satisfaction or that make such demands as the antiquarian-book trade, requiring the dealer to play at different times the rôles of detective, scholar, agent, psychologist and fortune-teller—quite apart from that of conventional buyer and salesman.

This book is concerned with all aspects of the world of anti-quarian books, with the books in demand, the people who dictate that demand, and the places where the two meet—the bookshop and the auction room. It looks at books that are rare because of their content, printing or binding, and books that will be in demand tomorrow because of the skill and love that have gone into their production today. The subject is vast and therefore its coverage necessarily superficial in places. Specialist books on collecting, binding, etc., are available to those who seek them. My concern is to interest and amuse as well as to encourage a desire for further study.

I wish to express my appreciation to Raymond O'Shea, of Baynton-Williams, for the assistance and advice given in the selection of the illustrations.

RHL

1 Booksellers and Collectors

With the twentieth century's ponderous, hiccoughing advance towards a classless society, we try even harder to slot people into socioeconomic pigeonholes. Society seems to be proud of the semblance of order it has attained, with its clearly defined blue- and white-collar workers, the professional men and the trades-men; all neat and tidy, as though careers automatically followed a predetermined pattern.

The antiquarian* bookseller, straddling trade and profession and vaguely identified with the arts, defies classification—if one attempted a job specification, the number of permutations would be daunting. What, then, do we look for? Well, if bookselling were pretentious enough to consider itself a profession, the standard prospectus handed to school or college leavers could concentrate on painting a picture of respectability, of erudition, and of an unparalleled knowledge of books. On the face of it, there is not much to quarrel with in that description: visualise the antiquarian booksellers you know, and the chances are that, in broad terms at least, they come close to fitting the bill.

My suggestion is that no one knows the required qualifications for antiquarian bookselling, principally because there is no standard model against which we can match our image. Take respect-

---

* There is no hard and fast definition of the term antiquarian and some purists dismiss anything post 1700 as merely secondhand, while a bookseller friend in San Antonio, Texas, complains that most of his customers define an antiquarian book as anything published before 1945. It has been suggested that 1830 is a reasonable demarcation line.

ability. With something of an axe to grind, I might be tempted to pretend that this quality is standard throughout the trade. But one has to concede there has been the occasional dealer who traded dishonestly enough to go to prison, and a few more who have erred, succumbing perhaps to a sudden agonising temptation. Yet the Antiquarian Booksellers Association guards its reputation jealously and there are those who would prefer prison to the wrath and contempt of their colleagues. So, all in all, there are and have been far fewer dishonest booksellers than there have been crooked 'professional' people. The greyer areas of morality —what one might describe as degrees of honesty—I will come back to later.

Meanwhile, 'respectability' in the broad sense of the word is a relatively recent attainment for booksellers. Samuel Johnson admitted to having been ashamed of his father, who ran a book-stall in various Midland towns, and Boswell later quoted him:

> Once indeed I was disobedient; I refused to attend my father in Uttoxeter market. Pride was the source of the refusal, and the remembrance of it was painful. A few years ago I desired to attone for this fault. I went to Uttoxeter in very bad weather, and stood for a considerable time bareheaded in the rain, on the spot where my father's stall used to stand.

Nevertheless, Dr Johnson came to respect his father—though not necessarily his trade, because he is reported to have made at least one physical attack, brandishing a book, on a bookseller.*

Books were not the only weapons used in such altercations. Several successful booksellers traded from the site of what is now Simmonds' bookshop in London's Fleet Street, including Bernard

---

* In fact, the instrument of his rage made its appearance at an auction in 1977, where the inscription inside the front cover of a heavy sixteenth-century Greek bible identified it as the volume Johnson had used to strike a Gray's Inn Gate bookseller called Thomas Osborne. 'He called Johnson a liar. That was too much. Johnson picked up the heaviest book to hand and hit Osborne across the side of the head and knocked him to the floor.' (The incident undoubtedly contributed to the current value of an otherwise undistinguished book; it fetched £480.)

Lintot (1675–1736), who established his reputation as the publisher of Alexander Pope. In those days booksellers were publishers too, which complicated life, and one of Lintot's successors in that shop, Jacob Robinson, is now remembered less for his business accomplishments than for the way he was treated by his customers. According to a report published in the *London Review* shortly after the death of the author David Hume, the latter was so incensed at the critical reception of his *Treatise of Human Nature* that he stormed into Robinson's shop demanding satisfaction:

It does not appear our author had acquired at this period of his life that command over his passions of which he afterwards makes his boast. His disappointment at the public reception of his Essay on *Human Nature* had, indeed, a violent affect on his passions in a particular instance, it not having dropped so dead-born from the press but that it was severely handled by the reviewers of those times in a publication entitled *The Works of the Learned*. A circumstance, this, which so highly provoked our young philosopher, that he flew into a violent rage to demand satisfaction of Jacob Robinson the publisher, whom he kept during the paroxysm of his anger, at his sword's point, trembling behind the counter, lest a period should be put to the life of a sober critic by a raving philosopher.

This is not to say that the tranquillity of the bookshop today is *never* disturbed. Peter Eaton, who will be remembered as the man who launched Britain's first 'stately home' bookshop (Lilies at Weedon in Buckinghamshire), recalls that, some years ago and in more humble circumstances, he had to placate an irate Dylan Thomas who threatened to 'tear the place apart'. Anyone who knew Dylan Thomas would accept that there was nothing personal in such an outburst!

On reflection, perhaps we have been confusing respect with respectability, so I might balance the issue by a brief reference to someone who earned the respect of his colleagues, despite his subsequent notoriety. Indeed, such is the inviolability of an *estab-*

lished reputation of respectability that the bizarre behaviour of the individual can have little impact on it.

Few of us who remember the infamous Peter and Hellen Kroger, convicted of spying for the Soviet Union less than twenty years ago, realise that Peter was an antiquarian bookseller in suburban Ruislip. (Ironically, one of his specialities was crime and the police!) Kroger was a popular figure in the book trade, although Frank Girdles, then head porter at Hodgson's Saleroom, says that he was always uneasy about the man's especially ingratiating manner. In fact, it was the Kroger stock, collated by Fred Snelling of Hodgson's over an eighteen-month period, that paid for the spy's defence. Mr Snelling was one of the first bookmen Kroger had met after his arrival in the UK in 1955—and he was probably the last he saw, in a prison visit on the Isle of Wight before the spy was sent back to Poland. Through the Krogers, Snelling also met Gordon Lonsdale, a senior officer in Soviet Intelligence and the head of the spy-ring, tried at the same time as the Krogers; and, subsequently, it was he who went to East Germany to negotiate Lonsdale's memoirs. The trade consoles itself with the knowledge that Peter Kroger does not really count; he was a bookseller and bibliophile only by inclination—espionage was his *real* profession.

So, if we accept that the average antiquarian bookseller is basically respectable, is he also erudite, the possessor of an unparalleled or at least a specialised professional knowledge? The answer is as indefinite as the length of a piece of string, especially as these are really separate issues. Dealing with the first, there are a dozen-and-one examples of men who have known nothing—and sometimes cared nothing—about books, but who have made small fortunes. So, quite obviously, at one end of the spectrum there is the scholar and at the other the semi-illiterate; and each has a rôle to play.

As for specialist 'professional' knowledge, what do we really mean? If we merely mean one who makes his living from the buying and selling of books, then we must concede at the outset that the specialist 'amateur' collector is often more knowledgeable about his subject than the man from whom he buys. But since the bookseller is principally concerned with making a profit from his knowledge, naturally he must know as much as possible about the product he handles. This is demonstrated in many ways.

Apart from flair or instinct, qualities which cannot be acquired, perhaps the two most important requirements are memory and contacts—or knowing where to get information and advice. These have little to do with academic learning, or even experience. Experience does have an important contribution to make to any man's business, but too often it merely reflects opportunities to repeat the same mistakes. The ability to memorise not only prices and basic information but also the backgrounds to scarce and rare items is invaluable, because a book-dealer should try not to depend too much on reference books—which are not infallible (in fact, until the 1950s many bibliographies and auction records were incomplete and occasionally inaccurate; some still are). All historical information must necessarily be secondhand to some extent, but the trouble with material falling into the hands of researchers is that original errors are invariably repeated by subsequent researchers, so that ultimately they become 'the truth'.

Raymond Kilgarriff of the Howes Bookshop, Hastings, one of Britain's leading stockists of scholarly books and also honorary librarian to the Antiquarian Booksellers Association, which provides a bibliographical research service to its members, admits to a conflict of attitudes: 'There is the viewpoint, to which I subscribe, that books have a romantic quality; and there is a tendency among certain pedants to destroy that romance by turning everything into an academic exercise.' But, dealing more and more with librarians and scholars, one has to be accurate, and the good bookseller will go to enormous lengths to achieve this end. In 1977, for example, Kilgarriff spent a couple of months of his 'spare' time on the preparation and research for a 2,392-item catalogue on *The Victorian Age*—yet the availability of a new reference book, *The Illustrator and the Book in England from 1790 to 1914*, by Gordon Ray, the American collector and authority, caused him, despite his own extensive knowledge, to reappraise his researches and in some cases make changes. One does not accept as gospel everything written, but it does not take long to decide which works have a contribution to make.

Descriptions must therefore be scrupulously accurate; an educated guess is not good enough. Even fairly deep research must be checked and double-checked. Ian Kidman, again of Howes Bookshop, once bought in a collection what appeared to be a set of *English Men of Letters*, edited by John Morley. Everything pointed to the fact that his 'set' of thirty-eight volumes was complete, including publisher's references and advertisements at the back of the books. However, in the process of cross-checking he found a book by John Gross (subsequently editor of the *Times Literary Supplement*) which indicated that there were in fact thirty-nine.

Nevertheless, reference books often do become a crutch. Most professional writers, by way of analogy, are apprehensive about dipping into a Thesaurus for inspiration, because of the danger of using it more and more, finishing up by desperately looking for alternatives to standard prepositions which have no practical alternative. This can be shattering to one's confidence, and confidence is essential to the good bookseller. Outstanding men like Charles Traylen of Guildford and J. N. Bartfield of New York have made their marks by knowing instinctively what they wanted to buy, while others dithered. Such men are not put off by record books, the bibles of so many to whom logic suggests: '£1000 is the top price ever paid for that item, therefore it would be foolhardy for me to go beyond that.' To Traylen and Bartfield, the record books are there to be changed; their philosophy is to anticipate trends, not to follow them.

The cliché 'unparalleled knowledge' has no application in bookselling; the parameters are too wide. Books are one cultural discipline, art another, yet art is only one of many subject classifications to the antiquarian bookseller. But, to him, art (English literature falls into the same category) does at least have visible horizons; moreover, the expert in this area would not necessarily be expected to know much about topography or natural history. Subjects like world history are not as easily contained, and all one can really hope to achieve is either a broad general knowledge or a mastery of one 'vertical' interest; such as a specific century or period in the development of one country or territory. The history of North America is like a drop in the ocean compared to that of the Middle East and the Orient, but so much of real significance is crammed into the past 250 years on that continent that American booksellers dealing in history tend to specialise in one specific aspect. If they concentrate on the Civil War, for example, they could easily slip up, if they relied purely on their own knowledge, while buying or selling a title associated with the pioneering days of the Old West. How could they be expected to know that a shabby little volume called *The Redemption of the Red Indian Savages by a Man of God* (Texas, 1820), rescued from a pile of junk, is almost priceless because (as the specialist collector might be able to tell them) only three copies were produced before the printer was scalped by Comanche Indians? They could not, perhaps, but they should be able to find out, which is where contacts come in.

Even so, practically every bookseller, in every country, has let 'treasures' slip through his fingers owing to ignorance. In some cases they should have known better, in others they could never have known. But this is part of the fascination for all of us, book lovers, collectors and dealers; why we all try to pick up 'bargains' (another relative expression), and why some trade and make their living from antiquarian books—depending on our degree of involvement and ability.

The philosophy of booksellers is also fascinating, because it has little to do with normal business practice. The person who is particularly astute at buying and selling, for example, will get by, but the chances are that those qualities would earn him greater rewards in other disciplines.

In some ways, though, the greater the love for books, the greater the handicap. If the bookseller spent as much time actually selling as he does impressing us with his fund of literary anecdotes, he would become more affluent, give it up, and become a collector. Furthermore, the bookseller tends to fall into the trap of not charging for his time and expertise. The lawyer and accountant will charge strictly on time spent, the medical man on opinion and treatment given, related to his time (although the psychiatrist, of course, has the best of both worlds!). The bookseller not only gives both time and advice free, he often gives them to potentially rival booksellers—the bibliophiles who will be sufficiently inspired to walk out and start a shop of their own. Indeed, when I was researching for my *Book Browser's Guide*, I encountered three bookdealers who had originally gone into the shop to buy a book and ended up by buying the business instead! On reflection, perhaps the original owners were better business-men than I have given them credit for . . .

At the 'top' end of the market, the responsibility for selection is seldom that of one man, although if he happens to be an entre-preneur his influence can be considerable, not only on his own business but on world prices. But the one- and two-man businesses still account for a significant part of the antiquarian-book world, and it is in these that one finds the greater variety of attitudes. More often than not, money is not the motivating force; indeed, if the proprietor accounted for his time—the hours spent buying and cataloguing after closing—as well as overheads, the profit element would often be shown as minimal. I am reminded of the time some years ago, when cinemas were hitting rock bottom, that I was interviewing a third-generation cinema owner who showed me his takings for the past year. The record was so gloomy that a few isolated weekly profits of a pound or two were occasions for rejoicing; when I asked why (and how) he continued, he replied: 'It's the only living I have . . .' What living? A number of booksellers come into this category, the pursuit of what they enjoy being more important than income.

But let us not cry over the misfortunes of the major-league bookdealer. A considerable amount of money passes through his cash register, and usually he manages to hang on to some of it. This brings us back to respectability and what is acceptable business practice. In most other trades, one buys at one price, adds a percentage to cover overheads and then sells at a rather higher figure for profit. Depending on the business this margin can be thirty per cent, fifty per cent, or as much as one hundred per cent. But as soon as one moves into the realm of scarce or rare material the sky is the limit, and percentages become irrelevant.

What is reasonable and what is extortionate? I am not qualified to say and, since the whole area of business ethics and morals is a very murky grey, I defy anyone to set standards acceptable to everyone in a trade as complex as this. All we can hope is that the person we are dealing with is honest at least fifty-one per cent of the time. The top antiquarian booksellers have reputations to protect and cannot afford to knowingly mislead a customer. But obviously it can happen, and the only answer is to establish a rapport with the booksellers of your choice and from then on back your judgement. The dealer is often more sinned against than sinner, and there have been many examples of collectors claiming that they were 'conned' because a price offered to them for an item was considerably lower than a quote from another dealer or auctioneer. Those old enough might recall an incident where the executors of celebrity X had been offered £1,500 for the great man's library and had indignantly refused—only to discover at a subsequent auction that the collection had netted a mere third of that amount.

I know booksellers who have bought a gem of a book for next to nothing, and, on obtaining a true valuation, have contacted the blissfully ignorant vendor to give him a more realistic proportion of the profit. The same dealer would perhaps think nothing of selling to a specialised collector for £2,500 a book he had picked up for £25—and be prepared to reveal the price he paid. Since a rare book is worth whatever someone is prepared to pay for it, who can say what is fair? In any case, what may seem more than fair in one situation might be regarded as devious in another. There are any number of anecdotes in the trade about veteran dealers who will lend or even give money to start a youngster up in business, and yet the following day screw him down on the price of stock. Other tales abound of hard-hearted dealers who have waived hundreds of pounds in commission on the sale of collections, their only concern being that the books ended up in the right hands.

In fairness it must be remembered that running an antiquarian bookshop is hardly the same as running a grocery store, where the proprietor can predict with some confidence that he must sell so many kilos of sugar a week to make it worth his while. Apart from the odd gem for which there is a waiting market, many volumes must necessarily remain on the shelves for many months (at today's cost of floor space, no small consideration). However, in general, booksellers I respect consider that they are entitled to make as much profit as possible when dealing with so-called equals, but that anyone exploiting that 'little old lady' is nothing more than a contemptible crook!

However, let us not become obsessed with prices, because a major problem today is not selling but *finding* material. There are different schools of thought about the desirability of actually selling really rare books, with, on the one hand, those who believe that almost irreplaceable books are worth far more than money can buy, and who may have rooms full of valuable material hidden away from customers' eyes; and, on the other, those who believe that a bookseller's duty is to maintain the supply of books on the market (regardless of cash-flow considerations).

Clearly, a rare book does not emerge every week, but the problem of finding 'available' copies has in recent years become acute. University libraries throughout the world have voracious appetites and, because of the increased demand, there is a greater tendency to hold on to the copy one had thought of selling. Perhaps it might be fairer to say that although very rare books do still appear—there have been several examples of extremely rare books (a Caxton, for example) not being seen for seventy-five years or so until three copies turn up within a few weeks of each other—prices are pushing them beyond the grasp of all but biggest purses.

It is, therefore, particularly tragic when books are destroyed by what the insurance companies call 'fire, tempest and riot' or 'malicious persons' motivated by political aims. In October 1976 the antiquarian stock of Emerald Isle Books in Belfast—probably the largest commercial collection in Northern Ireland—was blown up by IRA bombers; many treasures safeguarded for hundreds of years, and an integral part of Irish and English history, were destroyed in a split second. The Belfast store, a mecca for collectors of Irish history books and manuscripts from all over the world, had the misfortune of being next door to an Army observation post—which, to complete the devastation, collapsed on what remained of a great book collection. But the destruction of the books was no geographical accident, and as an act of 'ideological' barbarism must rank alongside the Nazi's ceremonial burning of books in the 1930s—except that the volumes lost in Ulster were mainly irreplaceable. Indeed, 44,000 were destroyed, including 10,000 rare items (part of a seven-ton container shipment) from one English college library, 5,000 volumes from a seventeenth-century seminary library in Germany, and 2,000 on Irish history. (Fortunately many other very rare Irish books were kept at other premises.) Destruction complete, the debris resembled a bibliophile's nightmare, with charred and soaked fragments of pages (bearing the names of distinguished printers such as Froben, Plantin, Keeberger and Aubriorum) from sixteenth- and seventeenth-century folios, many from the collection of the theologian and scientist Joseph Priestley.

The irony is that the number of rare antiquarian titles had been mounting steadily since the owner, John Gamble, closed the store in 1969 (making it 'by appointment only') to develop his catalogue business. The processing of four major catalogues a year in good 'ordinary' stock is time-consuming, and the rarer material was not sold with the same planned regularity.

In contrast with this barbarism, the reaction of other booksellers proved to be one of more than token sympathy. The Antiquarian Booksellers Association immediately made an offer of assistance—financial aid, storage accommodation or replacement stock—and as the news spread, unsolicited parcels of books began to arrive from booksellers who had previously been no more than names to the Gambles. The Gambles have kept nearly 400 letters from all over the Eastern and Western hemispheres, from both people in the trade and collectors: one particularly poignant but encouraging letter was sent by a leading Dutch antiquarian firm which described the way it had overcome similar misfortune—twice; the first when the owner's father had his stock destroyed in Germany during World War I, and the second when the current business was wrecked by the Germans in Holland in World War II. Books dealing with early Irish settlements in Brazil (written in Portuguese), and similar books in Spanish from the Argentine, arrived by air from booksellers in those countries, while others came from English firms and individuals—all without invoices, and all donors subsequently refusing payment.

This last incident, apart from offering an example of the interaction of inhumanity and compassion, serves to illustrate the risk of stockpiling valuable material for financial reasons, or because the books are rare. Stock, after all, can be destroyed by 'fire and tempest' as well as by bombs.

J. B. Bartfield of New York, one of the giants of the international book trade and a leading authority on illustrated works, never stockpiles books, let alone hides them. Bartfield, a self-made man who worked his way through college to qualify as a lawyer, has devoted his life to books. His business in Manhattan houses one of the best collections of colour-plate books in the United States, possibly the world, but he remains the true bibliophile, treating every copy he handles as an object of reverence, not just as merchandise. A beautiful book has an identity and personality comparable to that of a living entity, and Bartfield sees in his constant worldwide searching the thrill of the chase—a sport in which no one gets hurt. Once 'captured' the book is never held for long, being 'set free' to an appreciative collector. This may sound a little corny, but it is something he truly believes. Fortunately, there are still people who care, and one often sees booksellers visibly wince with discomfort at the way a beautiful book is being handled by a potential customer. (The same feeling lies behind the contempt expressed in the trade for those who buy old and imperfect editions of colour-plate books as 'breakers', selling the illustrations as prints and destroying the text.

Although this is not a book purely about booksellers, I make no apology for dwelling on them for so long because, while they obviously rely on customers to complete any transaction—and without the collector and the libraries, there would be no anti-quarian-book world—no one can deny that the booksellers are the catalysts. Indeed they are much more than that, and according to John Cowper Powys:

> . . . Every good bookseller is a multiple personality containing all the extremes of human feeling. He is an ascetic hermit, he is an erotic immoralist, he is a Papist, he is a Quaker, he is a communist, he is an anarchist, he is a savage iconoclast, he is a passionate worshipper of idols . . .

Although this is a vivid and in some ways very accurate description, there is a sector of the antiquarian trade, particularly at the top end, to which it most certainly does not apply; after all, Powys could not have anticipated trends. In much the same way as big business and its accounting arm took over Hollywood, so the antiquarian trade has been influenced by the entry of merchant banks and financiers. While usually remaining in the background, these faceless men nevertheless leave their mark. Certain famous names in bookselling might today be regarded as businessmen first and booksellers second, though, because of their background and tradition, they seem superficially little affected by the change. Business still comes to them automatically and some could possibly survive by relying solely on the ten per cent commission earned in representing libraries and institutions at auction sales.

It has been said that this representation at auctions does not require any special skill or experience—an assertion that would, of course, be strongly denied by many of the firms concerned, who argue justifiably that buying at an auction requires a high degree of skill and cannot be left in the hands of a junior who has been told in advance what the firm or the client have decreed their ceiling bids to be. A bookseller likes to *see* who he is bidding against because this knowledge can dictate his tactics; for example, it might prove cheaper to let the other man win on occasions, without pushing the price up too much, in the hope that he will sell the item to you later at a lower price than an auction 'duel' would have realised. Again, what happens if a client has been advised of a reasonable price, and the bidding goes higher than that? It is only when a bookseller has a rapport with a client that he knows instinctively when he can exceed his brief and pay more, sometimes considerably more. Equally, if his instincts are right and he buys, only to find that on this occasion the customer decides he cannot afford to exceed his limit, a dealer must be prepared to take the book into stock and feel confident that he will in due course sell it for a profit elsewhere.

In 1977, Quaritch, which represents many famous national libraries and institutions, bought some material at the first sale of the library of the seventeenth-century diarist John Evelyn; this

included a couple of prayer books for one client who had sentimental reasons for wanting them. Christies' estimated price was
moderate (up to £500 for the two) but Quaritch advised their
client that they might go for as much as £1,500. In fact, with the
auctioneer's additional (and still hotly disputed) commission from
the purchaser, the price eventually paid was over £5,000, which
indicates the elasticity of judgement a bookseller has to use. It is,
of course, the job of a bookseller at an auction to get the wanted
book or books for as little as possible; the job of the auctioneer to
get as high a price as possible.

But while there are established 'rules' and techniques in the
auction room, tactics can fly out the window in the heat of
battle. In the 1960s a first edition of Lewis Carroll's *Alice in
Wonderland* (Macmillan, 1885), purchased in an Indian bazaar for
1s 9d (9p), turned up at Hodgson's. The first edition of this book
is particularly valuable because of the circumstances of its publication. The author had paid for the publication and, when the
finished product was presented to him, he decided to everyone's
consternation that he did not like Sir John Tenniel's illustrations.
He ordered that they be done again (the book was eventually
published in 1886). But Macmillan had jumped the gun and already produced a few copies of the original, about thirteen of
which are known to be in existence. In view of its battered condition, Fred Snelling of Hodgson's estimated that their copy might
fetch only between £200 and £300, and received instructions
from a leading American bookseller to bid up to £500 on his
behalf. His brief was clear; '£500 is the absolute limit.' But at the
last moment the bookseller decided to put in an appearance and
became involved in a duel with a rival dealer. Not wanting to
come off the loser, he eventually paid £850 (ultimately selling the
book for £1,300).

Meanwhile, what about some of the characters on the other side
of the fence? The collectors, so many larger than life, even
stranger than fiction.

One does not have to be rich to be a collector, but it helps, and
many of the outstanding figures have been millionaires, men of
the stature of John Pierpoint Morgan, the US financier, whose

name is synonymous with twentieth-century capitalism. J. P. Morgan Junior (1867–1943) inherited his father's fortune and art collection, but came to international notice in his own right in World War I when he organised a New York bankers' syndicate with $100 million in gold. He acted for the British and French governments as agent for purchases in America, and for the US government when it entered the war in 1917. In his lifetime he gave $36 million to charitable and public institutions, including $15 million to the Pierpoint Museum Library, and $9 million to the Metropolitan Museum of Art. In 1933 he made over to trustees, as an institution to be used by the world's scholars, his magnificent library, valued at $8.5 million, housed in a superb marble building near the family residence. It contained about 25,000 volumes of illuminated manuscripts, early printed books, and examples of the work of famous presses. The library was featured in a fictional context (and as in Morgan's possession) in Ed Doctorow's 1970s bestseller *Ragtime*, when a grief-stricken negro musician and his anarchist disciples threatened to blow it up unless their demands were met.

But in terms of size it is difficult to conceive anything of the magnitude of the collection of Sir Thomas Phillipps (1792–1872). Had Sir Thomas been as sensible as the American financier about what was to happen to the collection after his death, it might never have been broken up, but conversely might never have received the attention it has had over the past century. Since 1886 at Sotheby's in London, the Bibliotheca Phillippica has been sold in stages, having attained over £3 million to date, with another ten years or so to go.

Much has been written about Sir Thomas, so I will confine myself to an outline of his collecting career, which he began at school at Rugby, before going to University College, Oxford (where he was awarded an MA in 1820). In fifty years he amassed the world's most famous private library, containing the greatest collection of unpublished historical manuscripts ever brought together by one man. It is estimated that he spent between £200,000 and £250,000, an incredible amount in those days, assembling some 60,000 manuscripts and over 50,000 printed books. Not only did he administer everything himself, but he catalogued and distributed to libraries all over the world details of nearly 24,000 books and manuscripts in his collection.

Sir Thomas called himself a 'vello-maniac' because of his obsession with manuscripts, which began when he read about the destruction of so many of them. Accordingly, he regarded their preservation through their purchase as a solemn duty, and even the inevitable rise in prices through his activities was calculated, since he believed it was another means of ensuring that manuscripts would not be destroyed through ignorance. Two of his particular interests were the history and literature of Wales and the preservation of public records: in 1848 he wrote to the Prime Minister suggesting that the records be housed in churches— thus converting bare walls into parish libraries.

During his lifetime Sir Thomas offered his collection to various institutions, including the British Museum and the Bodleian Library, for future literary research and as a lasting monument to his name, but the conditions he imposed were almost impossible. Even negotiations with an enthusiastic Disraeli, himself a man of literary accomplishments, for the collection to be bequeathed to the nation came to nothing because of his unrealistic terms. When he died in 1872, the library was bequeathed to his daughter Katherine (together with his coin collection, prints and pictures, and Thirlestane House, Cheltenham) on the condition that her husband, the Reverend John Fenwick, devote himself to the library. But the overheads of the mansion were so vast in relation to the inherited income (by the time various annuities and servants had been paid, Mrs Fenwick was drawing about £225 a year) that they could not even afford to insure its contents. Not only were the books almost priceless but also the art collection was of a superb standard, with many pictures by Sir Thomas Lawrence and George Catlin, including the latter's series on the North American Indians. The Settled Lands Act of 1882 and 1884 enabled trustees of 'chattels settled as heirlooms' to avoid certain restrictions hitherto imposed, and in 1885 the Court of Chancery granted Mrs Fenwick's request to sell the manuscripts and those printed books of which other editions or duplicate copies were present (as well as prints and coins).

Meanwhile, the most nationally relevant of the manuscripts

were being disposed of by private treaty to libraries all over the world, including the Pierpoint Morgan library. In World War II Thirlestane House was requisitioned and the books crated; after the war, because the house could no longer be used, arrangements were made for the sale *en bloc* of what remained of the library. Efforts to buy it for the United States were forestalled by the rare book firm of William H. Robinson, which traded from the premises in Pall Mall now occupied by Dawsons. The Robinson brothers, major figures in the antiquarian-book world at that time, managed to raise £100,000 to purchase Bibliotheca Phillippica in 1946, and transported it in a convoy of lorries, working day and night for a week, to London and the various sites where it was to be housed. Within ten years, the Robinson brothers had retired to begin devoting their time to examining and cataloguing the manuscripts and documents. Some were given away (the private papers of Sir Thomas, for example, to the Bodleian library) and the remaining bulk was gradually processed for sale at Sotheby's (see Chapter 7). Among the special bargains struck over the years was the purchase in 1935 for £4 5s od (£4.25) of a manuscript which proved to be Sir Walter Raleigh's commonplace book, written during his imprisonment and containing notes in preparation for his *History of the World*. Another lucky buyer paid all of £2 15s od (£2.75) for Petrarch's annotated copy of a fourteenth-century text of Valerius Maximus. (In 1977, Quaritch paid £5,000 for a single illustrated sheet from a fifteenth-century printing of Maximus—see Chapter 3.)

In terms of volume, perhaps the only comparable sale or shipment *en bloc* occurred with the splitting-up of part of the library of Sir Henry Wellcome, the founder of the drugs company, whose life reads like an adventure story. Through the Wellcome Foundation, he had amassed an incredible collection of principally medical and scientific books and, in the 1950s, he decided (mainly for space reasons) to get rid of all of the 'fringe' material. Once sorted at a warehouse in North London, this 'overflow' amounted to one million volumes—which the purchasers, Dawsons of Pall Mall, had to move in three monthly instalments.

As I said earlier, one does not have to be rich to collect intelligently, providing one is capable of exercising considerable self-control. I once received an order for out-of-print books from someone whose literary tastes were strangely diverse, though that in itself is not surprising. In due course one letter quoting some of the wanted material was intercepted by a desperate wife who phoned to beg that the order be discreetly lost or forgotten, complaining that her house was bulging at the seams with books her husband could not afford, and that even her essential housekeeping money was taken for more books. One hears of callous brutes who spend all their time in the pub, but who is to say that bibliomania cannot be just as cruel!

Most bibliomaniacs, as the name suggests, are obsessive to some degree. R. M. Williamson, in his *Bits from an Old Bookshop*, recalls a bookseller called Don Vincente who

> had a shop in Barcelona fifty years ago. His love for books became madness of a most extraordinary and terrible kind. When he sold a rare manuscript or book, he followed his customer and secretly stabbed him to death. He never took money from his victims, but murdered them for the sole purpose of regaining the books he had so recently sold.

Books as an investment are one thing, but no one can pretend that collecting is linked in any way with investment because no genuine collector ever dreams of selling—except in circumstances where he may no longer have control of his affairs. I have met at least one bookseller who has good reason to remember such a circumstance with affection, mingled with a certain sympathy for the vendor.

In 1960 Tom Emmett Henderson, a New York bookseller and publisher, was fortunate to encounter a retired electrical engineer who had invested in stocks successfully enough to indulge his hobby of collecting. 'Collecting', note: I did not specify books. The old man's interest happened to be books, but *collecting* was his obsession and, perhaps as an aftermath of his days as a tinkerer in all things electrical, this extended to light bulbs and screwdrivers!

Collecting books in his case meant looking for newly published titles in three main subject areas, natural history, science

and field sports. What made this collection unusual was that anything he considered worth buying (and his assessment of a book's
lasting value was invariably faultless) was worth having in mul-
tiples, between five and twenty copies, depending on his mood at
the time. It is not uncommon for enthusiasts to buy several
copies of a new title with the object of presenting spare ones to
friends, but this man had no intention of parting with a single
copy. Since they were all 'good' titles, the collection of around
70,000 books, sold shortly before the old man was committed to
an asylum, provided Tom Henderson with an income through
catalogues for the next ten years.

The sale—and books were only part of the hoard—was arranged by the old man's daughter, and luckily for her, fair prices
were paid since she dealt with buyers of integrity. But such was
the old man's compulsion that, after everything had been agreed,
he gathered up a brimming armful of books and announced to
anyone interested that these 'special items' had been withdrawn
for sentimental reasons. No one had the heart to stop him.

Not every collector is necessarily a hoarder. Andrew Lang in
his *Books and Bookmen* (1886) recalls Napoleon's compulsive
reading habits:

> He himself was one of the most voracious reader of novels that
> ever lived. He was always asking for the newest of the new,
> and, unfortunately, even the new romances of his period were
> hopelessly bad. Barbier, his librarian, had orders to send
> parcels of fresh fiction to his majesty wherever he might happen
> to be, and great loads of novels followed Napoleon to Germany,
> Spain, Italy, Russia.
>
> The conqueror was very hard to please. He read in his
> travelling carriage, and, after skimming a few pages, would
> throw a volume that bored him out of the window into the
> highway. He might have been tracked by his trail of romances,
> as was Hop-O'-my-Thumb, in the fairy tale, by the white
> stones he dropped behind him.
>
> Poor Barbier, who ministered to a passion for novels that
> demanded twenty volumes a day, was at his wit's end. He tried
> to foist on the Emperor the romances of the year before last;

but these Napoleon had generally read, and he refused, with imperial scorn, to look at them again. He ordered a travelling library of three thousand volumes to be made for him, but it was proved that the task could not be accomplished in less than six years. The expense, if only fifty copies of each example had been printed, would have amounted to more than six million francs. A roman emperor would not have allowed these considerations to stand in his way; but Napoleon, after all, was a modern. He contented himself with a selection of books conveniently small in shape, and packed in sumptuous cases . . .

Many specialist collectors know far more about their subject than the dealers, but for every expert there are a dozen eccentrics. In common with many booksellers I have a store of anecdotes about customers, but a couple of the most interesting come from the pen of Guido Orioli in his *Adventures of a Bookseller* (Chatto, 1938). Orioli is better known as the intimate friend and publisher of such distinguished writers as Norman Douglas, D. H. Lawrence, and Somerset Maugham, than for bookselling, which he seemed to regard as a spare-time activity between spells of globe-trotting. But it was as a bookseller that he met one customer who collected title pages.

The man, a Mr Merriam, claiming to be an authority on the history of printing, announced he was collecting title pages, partly for research, before writing a comprehensive history of printing. On first meeting Orioli he claimed to have over 2,000 pages—having thrown away the rest of the book in each case! When Orioli pointed out that any history of printing must incorporate incunabula (fifteenth-century works), which would not have had title pages, the collector was merely irritated at the disclosure of such unwanted and 'irrelevant' information. Later in Florence, Orioli actually saw Merriam's collection, consisting of several thousand title pages, of all sizes and periods, bound in beautiful volumes by a leading French bookbinder. Every page represented a book destroyed. (Which reminds me, most readers will know that the condition of a rare book is very important, and that 'missing' pages are a disappointment. But, quite apart from incunabula, books have been published on occasions without title pages, and many an expert has picked up a bargain by being in possession of this information when offered a 'crippled' copy.)

Another of Orioli's particularly fascinating customers was a blind beggar who would come to his Charing Cross Road bookshop before World War I to buy—and pay good money for—erotica, including separate drawings. When asked how he could appreciate such material he explained that his 'missus' described the illustrations so vividly, and read so well, that he could positively 'see' without eyes.

That blind man had the facility to conjure up pictures in his mind; others may want to make things disappear. Blackwells, of Oxford, once had a letter from a woman in Mexico who placed an order for books on invisibility. Nothing on the occult, she stipulated, just down-to-earth text books on how to scientifically induce invisibility. Since Blackwell's antiquarian department cares about its huge overseas mailing list, the letter could not be ignored, so a polite note was despatched apologising for the lack of material currently available—the books concerned having apparently vanished!

So the world of antiquarian books is a huge melting pot of people with differing philosophies and attitudes, of businessmen, of lovers of literature, art and beauty—and of just plain cranks. Show me a crank and I will show you a bibliomaniac to overshadow him. For example, I once told a bookseller the true story of a man who collected books on fleas. This subject is not unusual in itself, although I must admit I have never come across more than a handful of books on it. What was different about this man was that he would descend on his circle of bookshops at least once a week to demand: 'Anything new?' The bookseller responded to my anecdote by producing an eye-catching collection of books bound in army uniforms, and even more bizarre, the skins of different wild and domestic animals! So use the term 'crank' sparingly in the bookworld—you never know who you might be talking to!

2 'Generous Liberal-Minded Men'

To be an outstanding figure in the world of bookselling does not necessarily involve being financially successful: one cannot measure success in bookselling by the profits made. As I have said, if they had merely wanted to be rich, many booksellers would have chosen other trades. Yet some men are born to deal in books, and one could never imagine Gustave David (1860–1936), who ran a stall and shop in Cambridge for forty years, doing anything else. A hopeless businessman, David was nevertheless honoured twice by the University—the second time posthumously—for the contribution he had made to the humanities. In strictly commercial terms, however, all he bequeathed his family was a pile of debts.

A Parisian by birth, and the son of a secondhand bookseller, Gustave came to England in the 1870s, having already mastered three languages despite the lack of a formal education. He settled first in Gorleston, where he did what came naturally to him: he sold books. But he was constantly restless, and had moved to London by the time he was nineteen. Here he found the opportunity to really learn about antiquarian books and, with aptitude and prodigious application, he mastered the trade. Although by now an established bookseller, there was still something missing in his life: the rapport he was yet to attain with fellow bibliophiles. But in 1896 his fortunes changed suddenly when a horse-drawn dray stopped outside his shop in Red Lion Street. The incident which followed offers a clear illustration of fate playing its hand. Gustave David had no idea of its destination but on the dray were a number of cases, including a large portmanteau. Subconsciously drawn to it, he looked at the address on the label and vaguely recognised the name of a college in Cambridge. Unwittingly, an unknown undergraduate thus persuaded David that the university town, the great seat of learning, was the natural home for him and his books. The decision was instantaneous, and he left with all he had in the world—five pounds in books and cash.

In Cambridge, David started with a stall in Market Square (the shop alongside St Edward's Church was to come later), and for the next forty years he delighted academics and undergraduates not only with the books he produced for them but also with the warmth of his personality. He was fondly remembered as 'bringing a flavour of the Quais', although one literary figure used a similar expression in a less kindly context, remembering him principally for his 'unwashed' face. But Gustave was not just a quaint character. Much more accurate is the description in one of the obituary notices: 'He thought of his customers as his friends.' It was this empathy that nurtured his hitherto hidden qualities and produced the butterfly from the uncomfortable chrysalis.

David's sometimes volatile but at heart always gentle personality endeared him not only to his customers but also to the trade. Because of his naïvety as a businessman he was always in debt, but he never found himself short of credit. Nor did this naïvety affect his supply of books from sources like Quaritch who would have periodic clear-outs of what they, with their exceptionally high standards, would call 'imperfect' material. A tea-chest full of antiquarian books, valuable but for some minor damage, would be despatched to him, unseen, for twenty pounds. Many a volume would later find its way back to London in the possession of an undergraduate eager to capitalise on his bargain acquisition.

Thursdays would be spent in the London auction rooms, and on Friday mornings David would be besieged by his regulars, anxious to take their pick of the new stock as it was unpacked. A shrewder man would have refused to stand for this inadvertent harassment, but—either because he had not yet paid for the books and needed the cash or just because he liked to share his good fortune—David would let real 'treasures' go for merely a few pennies profit. Indeed, in the rush and confusion, he was sometimes lucky to get back what he had paid. Dealers often put the purchase price of their books in code inside the cover, but David used such a simple one, based on 'God Help Me' in German, *Got Helf Mir*, that over the years most of his customers knew what prices his letters represented (although the knowledge was irrelevant since his prices were always so low).

Another penalty of letting books go so quickly was that he seldom had time to examine the contents. One fortunate customer found, in a 1532 edition of *Simon Grynaeus*, the autograph of Sir Thomas More; another found a book containing a long inscription from Martin Luther. Make no mistake, David understood the books with which he dealt, but a happy customer was more important to him than the size of a profit margin. He was genuinely pleased when a customer found something he had missed, and philosophical about the more devious customers who considered they had put one over him—he knew that they would come back in search of other bargains.

The man's philosophy was summed up in an obituary by Dr W. H. D. Rouse in *The Cam* of January 1937 (coincidentally the first issue of this famous magazine):

. . . some of the finest and rarest of books have been on his stall. I remember the *Nuremberg Chronicle*, and what a fool I was not to buy it! Hakluyt from the first edition, Philemon Holland again and again, Ben Johnson's autographs . . . if he got a good bargain, he was pleased that some customer should do the same. He offered me one Saturday, a quarto *Dial of Princes*: 'You can have it for ten shillings,' he said, 'it is all scribbled over.' So it was; but I found on examining it the signature of Sir Thomas North* at the end, and all the corrections were in his handwriting. When I told David he was simply delighted. He generally spotted a name himself, but he never added to the price on that account. That book is now in the University Library, together with a *Cyropaedia* of Philemon Holland,† containing his autograph—I believe the only known autograph of

---

* Sixteenth-century translator.
† 1632 translation of Xenophon's work.

Holland . . . [even] his sixpenny and shilling stores were full of interesting books, such as you never see for sale anywhere.

But, as a businessman and a man with an obligation to support a family, he had his shortcomings. Anything unsold from the stall was put into a warehouse and, because he had no time to recycle it or issue catalogues, this stock mounted up so that by the time of his death (the day following another exhausting session at the London auctions) there were twenty tons of books piled high. This 'inheritance' was all the family had to pay off the small mountain of debts he had left. But his son, Hubert, who took over the business and managed to put it back on its feet, prefers to remember Gustave for his remarkable qualities, his enormous flair for antiquarian books, and his charming innocence (he said his prayers every night—in three languages). A man who knew and appreciated the masterpieces of the printed word, he spent his spare time reading popular novels, and was moved to tears by them. A modest man, he was rendered speechless with emotion in 1925 at the lunch in his honour at Trinity College, in recognition of the 'conspicuous services he has rendered the cause of Humane Letters'. Shortly after his death, Cambridge University Press published a small volume of appreciation compiled from the tributes of distinguished men of letters, including Sir Arthur Quiller-Couch.

Part of David's immense popularity could be attributed to the very fact that he *was* a hopeless businessman, since most successful men inevitably alienate a number of people along the way. But someone who was not only a first-rate businessman but, according to an obituary in the *Daily Telegraph*, 'the King of booksellers . . . Napoleon of the sale room . . . incomparably the greatest, wisest, best informed, most liberal and munificent bookseller of his age, or any age', was Bernard Quaritch (1819–99). That is not to say that Quaritch never had financial headaches. Still in the possession of the firm he founded are his accounts for 1847, the first year he went into business on his own. Written at the side of his neat entries is the salutary note: : 'According to these calculations I am insolvent.' It has been suggested that Quaritch leaned heavily on knowledgeable clerks, but this is really nit-picking, because of that special quality he shared with other great booksellers—men like J. N. Bartfield, Charles Traylen, Frank Hammond of Dawsons, Martin Breslauer and another American, L. D. Feldman, known as El Dieff—an entrepreneural instinct, or flair, for *knowing* when to go over the odds. He may not have been a scholar in the accepted sense, but he was a highly literate man.

Born in Prussia on 23 April (students of astrology will note the connection with Shakespeare), he was studying Greek, Latin and French by the age of nine. At fifteen he was apprenticed to a bookseller, winning his spurs in Berlin before coming to England in 1842 with just two letters of introduction—one to the publisher John Murray (an important figure in those days) and one to Henry G. Bohn, London's leading secondhand bookseller. They both turned him down but two more years of diversified experience with a noted bookseller in Paris encouraged him to announce to Bohn, 'You are the first bookseller in England. I mean to become the first in Europe.' Mrs Bohn is reported to have agreed with that prediction.

Having embarked on his own account, with capital of well under a hundred pounds, Quaritch launched his first catalogue, published in broadsheet and entitled *Quaritch's Cheap Book Circular: selling for cash at very reduced prices*, which ranged from a shilling to a guinea. He was later to produce the greatest booksellers' catalogues ever seen. By 1858 he had stepped up in class, in that year buying his first Mazarin bible for £596. Nearly thirty years later he bought the same copy back for £2,650 to resell; it eventually went to the United States in 1923 for £9,500. But even in those early days he was able to anticipate demand. Towards the end of the 1850s, with the threat of war in the East, he started publishing Turkish, Persian, Arabic, and even Chinese grammars and dictionaries. He also cornered the market in Korans, selling a considerable number to Cairo, then capital of to Arab world.

In 1860 he moved to Piccadilly, becoming friendly with men of distinction, including Disraeli, Gladstone (a customer from his Castle Street days thirteen years earlier), Sir Henry Irving, Ellen Terry and Sir Richard Burton. At this period he was beginning to dabble in publishing; in 1861 he published *Translations from the Greek*, by Gladstone and his brother-in-law Lord Lyttleton, to commemorate the silver weddings of the two men, who had married sisters. Among his later publishing ventures were William Morris' 'Saga Library', translations of the Icelandic sagas on which Morris worked with the scholar Magnusson, and four of the Kelmscott Press titles.

Quaritch's reputation as a buyer spread beyond the book world. People would go just to watch him in action at important sales, often commenting on his *'audace, encore de l'audace, et toujours de l'audace'*. And although he was remembered mainly for the scale of his buying, he was often more excited by some of the 'novel' items he was able to acquire. At the sale of the Didot library at Paris in 1879, for example, he obtained a manuscript prayer book that had belonged to Sir John Talbot, first Earl of Shrewsbury, containing a number of pieces of devotional poetry written by him during his capture by Joan of Arc in 1429, which he appears to have carried with him until his death in battle in 1453, when he was over eighty. Quaritch also bought, and sold for £1,600, the first letter from Columbus to King Ferdinand and Isabella announcing the discovery of America, printed on two leaves at Barcelona in 1493.

His catalogues had become increasingly impressive, and 1874 saw a masterpiece of scholarship—1,889 pages containing 23,000 titles, all valuable books and manuscripts, classified and accompanied by an index of 109 pages in three columns. It was described by Quaritch as 'the greatest effort of my life', yet was followed three years later by a 'supplementary' catalogue, comprising monthly sections totalling 1,672 pages. His last great catalogue, still used as a work of reference by booksellers and librarians, and completed in 1888, contained 38,552 items on 4,066 pages, with the index published in 1892 having 427 pages in three columns.

The extent to which he dominated the trade in the last twenty years of the nineteenth century (he died in December 1899) is illustrated by the following purchases: over £33,000 worth of £56,000 from the sale of the Sunderland library of Blenheim Palace; over £44,000 of £86,000 from the sale of the Hamilton Palace library; while at the sale of the Osterley Park library he bought nine out of eleven Caxtons. Among the tributes on his death was this one from the London *Times*:

> It would scarcely be rash to say that Quaritch was the greatest bookseller who ever lived. His ideals were so high, his eye so keen, his transactions were so collosal, his courage so dauntless, that he stands out among men who have dealt in old literature as a Napoleon or a Wellington stand out among generals. Like Napoleon too, he rose from small beginnings, and owed his success entirely to his own intelligence, aided by the circumstances of his time.

The *New York Times* added:

> For the best part of half a century, Bernard Quaritch held his position as the greatest dealer in old books in the world. His word was law so far as the value or rarity of a volume was concerned. It is no exageration to say that he made in great measure the modern market for scarce books.

The firm of Quaritch remains perhaps the best known name in antiquarian books (in 1951 it bought the Gutenberg Bible which subsequently sold for a million pounds) and many of its directors have themselves been men of distinction in the book world, but nothing can fill the void left by men of such giant stature as its founder.

Another Napoleon of the auction room, like Quaritch a self-educated man, is Charles W. Traylen, Europe's leading authority on the illustrated book.* Charles Traylen is a man who dictates trends and buying patterns, these days through the saleroom but earlier in his career through an ability to anticipate demand and

---

* Perhaps I should qualify the word 'authority' because, in this age of specialisation, there are a number of very knowledgeable men and women who can tell you in an instant not only *when* an artist worked on a subject but also *why* he used red for one edition and maroon in another. But the true definition of 'authority' is 'power, or right to enforce obedience'.

initiate what were then controversial selling techniques. He left school at fifteen and, after working briefly as an errand boy, displayed some of the initiative that was to serve him so well by starting his own bicycle business, buying old machines for a few pence and renovating them for re-sale. He might have been a rich man today except that in 1920 his mother found him a job with the Cambridge booksellers Galloway & Porter at 7s 6d (37½p) a week. The shop had, in only fifteen years, acquired considerable prestige through the abilities of Charles Porter, a founder member of the Antiquarian Booksellers' Association (his son George, who joined the firm the same time as young Traylen, was to become President of the Association between 1970 and 1971). A university-town bookshop—and not very many of these still sell antiquarian and secondhand books—is undoubtedly the best place to acquire a grounding in classical and scholarly works, and to learn the value of the Greek and Latin classics. Young Charles learned fast, and eventually left to become manager of another distinguished firm, Thomas Thorp of Guildford, perhaps tempted by a salary increase of 10s (50p), to bring him the princely sum of five pounds a week.

Towards the end of the 1930s, Traylen foresaw that beautifully illustrated books would rise in value more dramatically than any other type. Between 1938 and 1940 Gould's *Birds of Great Britain* (five volumes) would fetch £25, and Gould's *Humming Birds* (six volumes) £75. (John Gould, 1804–81, is considered the outstanding illustrator of birds, alongside John James Audubon, 1780–1851, who specialised in North American birds.) Traylen put an advertisement in the London *Times* offering to pay £30 and £100 respectively for the works. The action alarmed his employer and caused consternation in the trade, which complained that offering 'over the odds' did not constitute fair business competition. The advertisements had the desired effect, however, attracting over the next few years not only the sets actually requested but other valuable 'incidental' material as well. Among the treasures Traylen picked up at this time was a set of the limited subscriber edition of *Humming Birds* for £150, which he fondly remembers as the finest set he has ever seen—much better, in fact, than another set sold some years later for £22,000. Yet he returned on that occasion to face a worried Mr Thorp, who complained that the most they had ever received for a set was £100. A day later Traylen reassured him, finding a customer for £250.

In October 1945 he set up on his own, starting as he expected to continue. On his very first outing, which he might have been expected to approach with caution, he paid the highest price of the day for a set of Dickens bound in fine (according to him, 'flashy') morocco, selling it two days later to someone who wanted it principally for display.

Indeed, while I have already referred to his foresight and courage, another of his qualities admired by the big names in the trade is 'taste'. Traylen shrugs this off, maintaining that he merely likes to buy the best copies available, advising that one should 'never have to apologise for the condition of a book'. Nor is he a literary snob. There is something for all bibliophiles, including a 5p tray, in his shop, which stands in the shadow of Guildford castle, near the house in which Lewis Carroll died in 1898. He regards only 10,000 out of a stock of 50,000 as really fine books, and on one occasion he supplied a Japanese firm with an order for two items: a Kelmscott Chaucer for £2,000, and an Everyman Library title for 25p!

At an auction, two weeks after leaving Thorp's, he was attracted by an Audubon's *Birds of America*.* On this occasion only Volume One was available and the plates had been folded, so that the trade was cautious. Not so Traylen, who paid £2,800 of his own money at a time when he was still really finding his feet. Again his judgement was vindicated. The following morning, someone telephoned to offer him a 'small' but quick profit. Most men would happily have accepted two or three hundred pounds' profit, but Charles demanded £4,000 *and* a decision by 11.15 a.m. the same morning. The offer was accepted and the book went straight from Sotheby's to the new owner.

Charles Traylen built his reputation on his courage to buy

---

* Audubon is indisputably the most sought-after bird illustrator, and in 1976 this title, a limited edition with hand-coloured plates, changed hands for $352,000—the highest figure ever reached at a book auction (until 1977 when another copy was sold for £216,393).

while others paused to recoup their expenditure along the way. In the ten years after the war, when antiquarian books were in plentiful supply, he was probably the only one of his contemporaries who went out to buy every day—admittedly with the help of a bank manager who had faith in him. His selling philosophy is contrary to that of most booksellers who, having spent a hundred pounds, sell off two or three good titles to pay for the new purchases. Traylen sells the 'junk' first and keeps the good ones until he can get a fitting price. Another piece of advice—and one that booksellers can learn from collectors, who admittedly do not have to worry about profit margins—is 'sell, to enable you to buy better books next time, and then continue the process—not the other way round'.

While the business has grown substantially, Traylen still has a staff of only six—two of whom have been with him for over twenty years—because he has no wish to expand; a policy decision easier to understand in the book trade than in other businesses. The question of size in the antiquarian book business is a provocative one. There are those who, without taking anything away from Traylen, nevertheless say: 'But he has only himself, and his money, to worry about. No board of directors, or shareholders, breathing down his neck, aghast at the resources he is tying up in one purchase.' Equally without rancour, Charles says of the big firms: 'It's easy to splash out when you're not reaching into your own pocket.'

Today he buys only what he wants—and when he wants something he usually gets it. There are countless examples of Traylen's purchasing power. In 1977, for example, on the first day of the John Evelyn sale he paid the highest amount of the day, £18,000, for a 1661 edition of a New Testament Bible translated into Amerindian (to be precise Algonquin), when the estimated price was between £10,000 and £15,000. The book was one of only forty copies published for presentation in North America, and was given to Evelyn by Robert Boyle, chief officer of the Corporation for the Propogation of the Gospel Amongst the Indians. Another day when I met him for a drink he had just spent an 'uninteresting' morning at an auction, picking up a Nuremberg Chronicle for £7,000. (With certain notable exceptions, the sons of outstanding men seldom attain the same heights, and although bookselling's famous names have survived it has usually been through 'imported' talent. But it has been suggested that Charles Traylen's son Nigel, who runs Beeleigh Abbey books, owned by Foyles, is a chip off the old block.)

Before leaving Traylen, here is one anecdote from many in his fifty years in the business. In 1947 he sold to a grateful State Archives the original 1663 charter for Carolina, but the circumstances behind the sale are remarkable. The story began in 1945, in his first year of business at Guildford, when he bought some books from a Captain Howes for £14, £2 more than the highest offer from London dealers. Six months later, an appreciative customer reappeared with some more books and a rolled up vellum scroll, which he had bought for 9s (45p) in a lot that included a washstand and sundry other items. Not knowing its true value, Traylen paid him £25, with the promise of more to come should it prove valuable (the man was in fact to get another £500 six years later). Because of the pressure of developing a new business, the charter was put on one side, and it was a year later that Traylen was looking at an eighteenth-century travel book on the early days of America, which happened to deal with the State charters, when he recognised the one in his possession.

The irony is that a mere three months before the charter, together with the contents of a house in Hertfordshire (home of Lady Clinton-Baker), had been auctioned, Traylen had been called in to appraise a collection of books in the wine cellars. He bought three tons of books, none of particular interest, but had not gone into the house itself, where the charter was lying unrecognised.

In 1947 it went into an American catalogue at £2,500 ($10,000 at that time) and was snapped up by the State Archives of North Carolina, on approval. Actually getting paid was beset with complications through the fault of no one. Expected funds did not materialise, and although Traylen might have found another buyer he offered the State time to pay. Then the pound was devalued, dropping from $4 to $2.80 which meant (having invoiced in sterling) a further headache. However, the account was eventually settled two years later, with ten per cent compensatory interest. Today the charter must be worth more than $100,000. The footnote to the story is that Charles Traylen was invited to the Tercentenary celebrations at Raleigh, in North Carolina in 1963, where he was fêted and awarded a commemorative medal. Not the most expensive antiquarian item to pass through his hands, but perhaps one of the most interesting.

An historical document is not, however, an automatic pass to the freedom of a city or state, as other booksellers have discovered. Charles P. Everitt, an experienced American bookseller whose sixty years in the trade ended shortly after he had completed his memoirs, *The Adventures of a Treasure Hunter* (1951), recalls getting the cold shoulder from the State of Idaho. What he had was admittedly not quite of the magnitude of a State charter, but it was a document of considerable historical importance—an original pencil sketch of the Coat of Arms of Idaho by the Governor of the time. He catalogued it:

> Lyons, Caleb. Original pencil sketch of the Arms (Seal) of the Territory of Idaho (1866). Lyons, Gov. Caleb. A.L.S. describing the Coat of Arms . . . adding "By the authority in me vested by an Act of the Legislature, passed hereby adopted I have designed above described Coat of Arms . . ." 1 page (1866) E. R. Howlett. Certificate of adoption and reproduction of Seal, April 20, 1866. Three pieces. $350.

When the State was approached no one, from the Governor down, was interested—for a multitude of reasons, including the fact that since they already had copies they did not need the original! A local newspaper editor suggested that Caleb Lyons had been a rogue and scoundrel, and that no one would pay 350 *cents* for anything of his, except perhaps his scalp. Eventually it was suggested that the State might be prepared to refund the postage if Everitt donated the documents. Fortunately for him, a collector of Western Americana, amused at Everitt's catalogue plea 'Is Idaho Only Interested in Potatoes?' eventually took them off his hands.

A man who over the years has backed his judgement even more

dramatically than Charles Traylen is J. N. Bartfield, whose Manhattan bookstore houses one of the best collections of colour-plate books in the United States, and could make a similar claim for beautiful bindings. In 1966, Bartfield startled the trade by taking the bidding to $60,000 for the rare four-volume Audubon (1827–38)—approximately three times the top price previously paid. If they believed he was audacious then, they must have thought he had really overstepped the mark four years later when he bought another set for £90,000; but, of course, he had no trouble in selling them. That sort of confidence was justified when, in 1976 at Christies' New York establishment, an Audubon from the collection of the late Grace Phillips Johnson was acquired by Didieu, the New Orleans dealer, for a world-record price of $352,000, $100,000 over the highest pre-sale estimate. That record for a printed book was broken a year later at the same auction room when Bartfield again topped the bidding for another Audubon *Birds of America*, property of the late Carrie S. Beinecke with £216,393.

Again a self-made man, Jack Bartfield, now in his middle sixties, travels the world in search of books. There was never much doubt that he was destined to be a bookseller because, although he practised law until 1937, even when at college he was paying his way by working for an antiquarian-book trade paper. Apart from the flair he has in common with other outstanding book-men, it has been suggested that one of his special qualities is single-mindedness. His manager, George Murray, who has spent nearly thirty years in the business, recalls an occasion when they went to look at a collection of books left by a college professor who, to be near the faculty, had lived in a slum area, one of the toughest parts of New York. Murray's apprehensions over an evil-looking landlord evaporated at the sight of a much more fearsome hound which had followed its master to the door. A third bookseller, who had acted as intermediary, decided there and then, as the dog strained at its leash to get at them, that discretion was the better part of valour. Confidence waning, Murray nevertheless gritted his teeth and entered the apartment. To reassure himself he jokingly enquired whether the dog were really as vicious as it looked. Even as he posed the question it did not seem particularly witty, and when the landlord, much more seriously, replied that it was more dangerous than it looked, and that any moment they might become next in a long line of mangled victims, his nerve finally cracked. Murray waited in the street and, much later, Bartfield emerged, having bought the collection, blissfully unaware of the tensions and the disappearance of his colleague. Dog? What dog?

Bartfield and Murray are men who love books, and respond to that quality in others. A student with only a few dollars to spend will get more attention, if his interests are genuine, than a customer intending to buy leather sets as an investment. Bartfield has proved to be exceptionally generous to bibliophiles he respects. On one occasion, a Bible that had belonged to the English Royal family, with photographs of the Holy Land by Frith, and therefore worth several thousand dollars, was actually given to a customer who admired it. Cynics would say that the customer probably paid in other ways, but I do not believe this to be the case. Generosity linked to integrity is a rare combination that cannot be lightly dismissed.

Earlier I mentioned the need to establish a rapport with and to trust a bookseller; this is aptly illustrated by the care taken by one of the young ladies who work for Bartfield. She has a customer she never sees, yet the man has complete confidence not only in her honesty and judgement but also in her taste. 'You know what I like,' he wrote, some years back. 'Send me a book a month using your judgement—then I can always look forward to a surprise.' The books despatched each cost approximately $100 and, as with most reputable booksellers, are sent 'on approval'. At the time of publication of this book she has had not one returned.

Audacity, courage, knowledge and even taste have been mentioned. The entrepreneur is also a trend-setter, not only in prices and fashion but in ideas; consequently he is usually an innovator in more than one area. Remainders (books sold cheaply by publishers for various reasons) are commonly considered to be a post-war phenomenon, but in fact they were pioneered 200 years ago by a London bookseller, James Lackington, who resisted the traditional practice of destroying half or even three quarters of his leftover stock in order to charge full publication price on what was left. He defied the wrath of the trade by instead selling them off at one half or one quarter of the retail price. In 1791 he estimated that four times the number of books were being sold as had been twenty years before. (Incidentally, remainders frequently rise above their original price when the public belatedly recognises their true value, and some eventually become collectors' items. An early example was the ten-volume *Some Account of the English Stage 1660–1830*, by the Reverend John Genest, published in 1832 at £5 5s od (£5.25). At the time, sets had to be given away for £1 10s od (£1.50); today they are worth many hundreds of pounds.)

Lackington also recognised the potential, and became involved in, book clubs and libraries, which were resisted by the establishment as serious threats to the existence of ordinary booksellers. But he stuck to his guns in all matters and invariably won the day. He even anticipated the Foyles and Blackwells of the present day by opening a vast book emporium in London (although his modern counterparts built their operation by degrees). Lackington's book centre, in Finsbury Square, Moorgate, was pictured by Charles Knight in his *Shadows of the Old Booksellers* (1865) following a visit the author had paid to the so-called 'Temple of the Muses' in 1801, when he was only ten:

A dome rises from the centre, on top of which a flag is flying. This royal manifestation proclaims that this is no ordinary commercial establishment. Over the principal entrance is inscribed 'Cheapest Booksellers in the World' . . .

We enter the vast arena, whose dimensions are to be measured by the assertion that a coach and six might be driven round it. In the centre is an enormous circular counter, within which stand the dispensers of knowledge, ready to wait upon the country clergyman, in his wig and shovel hat; upon the fine ladies, in feathers and trains, or upon booksellers' collector, with his dirty bag . . .

We ascend a broad staircase, which leads to 'The Lounging Rooms', and to the first of a series of circular galleries, lighted from the lantern of the dome, which also lights the ground floor. Hundreds, even thousands of volumes are displayed on shelves running round their walls. As we mount higher and higher, we find commoner books, in shabbier bindings; but there is still the same order preserved, each book being numbered according to a printed catalogue.

Lackington's achievement at the end of the eighteenth century is put into perspective when one considers that probably two thirds of the books around today have been published in the past forty years.

Two men today associated with selling books *en masse* are Peter Eaton, and Richard Booth. Booth runs at Hay-on-Wye, Powys, Wales, probably the world's largest 'bookshop' and certainly the most publicised because of the novelty of the concept of taking over almost an entire village. In creating a cottage industry of books, Booth has put Hay-on-Wye on the map—and anything that encourages people to talk and think about books is surely a good thing.

Yet he has a number of critics within the trade. It is said, for a start, that he 'borrowed' the idea of a multiplicity of shops in one area from another bookseller. But then many of us have first-class ideas from time to time and do nothing about them. Booth backed his hunch, and no one can deny that he chose an excellent location, within easy reach of everyone from the south and centre of Wales to the heavily populated areas of England, around Bristol and the West Midlands.

There are also countless stories, recounted with glee by 'knowledgeable' booksellers, of rare volumes picked up for a song because Booth 'knows nothing'. But this is hardly fair, since booksellers have always lived partly through scoring off each other in specialist areas.

Booth chooses to operate by buying and selling in bulk, and is concerned less with the trade than with potentially big buyers such as librarians. He attracts them by catering for their needs, with the symposium, with accommodation for overnight stops, and so on. In some ways he might be described more as a marketing man than a bookseller. His approach is technically sound.

While others buy a collection in order to obtain two or three valuable items, Booth reckons that every book has an audience if one has the time to identify it. His answer is 'horizontal selling': he breaks down new stock into subject collections, within the framework of which even relatively worthless books acquire some value, or he creates saleable units. Mind you, I think it is fair to say that this is generally overdone these days, and that there are probably too many spurious collections being formed all over the place. However, Booth obviously finds it pays, and accordingly has less time than most to look for the odd treasures among his purchases. Approve or not, unquestionably he will be remembered when other, 'better', booksellers have long since been forgotton.

In contrast, Peter Eaton, who also buys two or three thousand books a week, is a bookseller of the traditional school, although very much an individualist and idiosyncratic enough to have his cluster of critics too. A man of strong principles, he often seems to swim against the tide. A conscientious objector during World War II, his respect of animal as well as human life was illustrated when he bought Lilies, a sixty-room country mansion, at Weedon in Buckinghamshire, heart of fox-hunting country, and immediately banned the local hunt from entering his extensive grounds. Dealing less in rare works than in 'general' antiquarian and secondhand material, Eaton is interested more in the content of a book than in its appearance in aesthetic terms. In common with many booksellers, he is inclined to sell off cheaply stock that has interested him less to make room for material he considers more important; but in his case it is the very much in-vogue illustrated and children's books that go out quickly. It is no coincidence that a bookseller's personal interests are often reflected in his business speciality: Charles Traylen, the authority on illustrated items, has a vast collection of children's books, partly because they remind him of his happy childhood and partly because of the illustrations. Peter Eaton, however, collects sociology of the 1840s, and his knowledge of this subject is extensive.

Having been a bookseller for thirty years, Eaton's fortunes have fluctuated with the various trends and fashions. He has, in fact, picked up ephemera, particularly paintings, for next-to-nothing and watched them become very valuable, although these are personal items not intended for re-sale. On the other hand he has occasionally bought and sold items long before they had a chance to appreciate.

Early in his career, during his first dealings with 'celebrities', he bought a number of books belonging to Queen Victoria, all with signatures and inscriptions in her handwriting. Today, they could be worth a considerable sum of money; at the time there was little interest either in her or in the Victorian era. The opportunity to acquire them came when he was invited to Kensington Palace by Princess Alice and the Duke of Connaught, who used to buy military books from him. As Quaritch and others had discovered before him, an interest in books is a great social leveller.

Trained as a printer, Eaton had started with a barrow in London's famous Portobello Road market; he graduated to a small shop in Kensington Church Street, which was very fashionable just after World War II and became a mecca for people in the arts. Apart from a volatile Dylan Thomas, other talented writers who became customers included Nina Hamnet who wrote *The Laughing Torso*, remembered less for her wit or intelligence than for her disconcerting habit of keeping her money in her stocking tops. Eventually Eaton moved on to Holland Park, converting what had been adjoining shops before 1974 into possibly London's first purpose-built bookshop in fifty years. Meanwhile, Lilies had been opened, housing half a million volumes in a unique setting, the house itself decorated with pre-Raphaelite paintings and drawings, and many *objets d'art* of superb taste.

For his area of bookselling, Eaton considers the essential qualities to be a gambling instinct, business aggression and creative talent. The last may seem a little surprising, yet is has contributed to the styles of a number of good booksellers. One can often start with an obscure book which means nothing to anyone, only to find that a little research into the author, or subject, produces a demand. The brochures of 'creative' booksellers like the late Peter Murray-Hill and Ben Weinreb of Weinreb & Douwma, who literally single-handed initiated today's enormous interest in architecture, and who claims to sell 'reborn ideas' rather than books, make fascinating reading in their own right. This obviously also applies to the beautiful illustrated catalogues of many leading booksellers and auction houses, but these are not so much creative as scholarly works of reference.

One example of Eaton's style of cataloguing is his description of a lot of some 170 letters written between 1875 and 1910, either by or about a little known Colonel George Wingate, who served for more than thirty years in the British army in India. Eaton uses extracts from these to sketch the three significant features of the Colonel's character and military career: his altercations and differences of opinion with authority, his fervent religious beliefs (he and his wife were Plymouth Brethren) and his love of the army. If those symbols of Bible and sword are familiar, you will not be surprised to learn that the fiery 'unknown' soldier was the father of the brilliant and unorthodox General Orde Wingate who, in World War II, defeated the 'invincible' Japanese soldier in jungle warfare, and who for religious reasons trained and inspired the underground Jewish army, the Haganah, so laying the foundations for Israeli military supremacy in the Middle East. Obvious as this example might be, it serves to explain why Eaton believes that the profit margin in a transaction is almost an irrelevance, since a book is worth *nothing* until one creates a demand and finds someone willing to pay for it.

If he has a speciality it is in manuscripts and association copies*, and his interest in the subject has provided some happy memories. He once found an original Ruskin drawing in an association copy of educational interest, which he had bought because one owner had been the author and scholar Samuel Robinson, and another W. H. Hereford, scholar and early advocate of opening universities to women. Back home, Eaton was examining it when out fell the drawing by Ruskin, which went straight into his personal collection!

Among the interesting collections which have passed through Eaton's hands over the years are the library of George Bernard Shaw, including Grove's *Dictionary of Music and Musicians* (Shaw

---

* As the name suggests, copies of interest because of their association with someone, more than because of their content.

(*above*) Charles Traylen

(*above right*) Peter Eaton

(*right*) Bernard Quaritch (1819–99)

(*right*) Gustave David (1860–1936), from a drawing by Sir William Nicholson, used to illustrate the book of tributes published in 1937. (*Courtesy of Cambridge University Press*)

(*below*) James Lackington (1746–1816)

(*below right*) Wynkyn de Worde (1493–1534)

was once a music critic) with the writer's tiny handwritten notes on the fore-edge; the museum of Marie Stopes, pioneer of birth control; H. G. Wells' books on that subject; and a collection of nearly 1,700 books, manuscripts, journals and letters relating to Havelock Ellis and others, emanating from two sources, the British Sexological Society and the Eugenics Society.

However, any suggestion that the ranks of outstanding booksellers are populated only by men who deal in books by the million, or in matching monetary values, would be a distortion. There are a select few who maintain what in publicity jargon is a 'low profile', men who may not attempt to dominate the auction room or dazzle us with their catalogues, but who nevertheless earn the ungrudging respect and admiration of their colleagues. And in selecting booksellers who could qualify for the description 'outstanding', a thorny problem encountered was to evaluate the specialists known to only a small section of bibliophiles—men like Roderick Brinkman of Toronto, whose shop, Monk Bretton Books, has been described as the best in Canada. Yet being best in that country would not automatically qualify it for the same rating in Europe. As it happens, Brinkman probably is at the very top in his speciality, the private presses, but if one takes in this vertical interest one would then have to introduce outstanding specialists in other equally limited areas.

One man who might be classified as a specialist, but in the very broad field of fine books, is Colin Franklin of Culham, Oxford, who entered the business after twenty years in publishing, having made his mark as managing director of one of the largest British firms. When I was researching certain parts of this book it was his name which constantly cropped up among other authoritative sources—'You have spoken to Colin Franklin, of course?'—and the respect in which he is held is not really related to his success or to his undeniable knowledge, but rather to his distinctive philosophy. Denying all suggestions that he is in any way different, Franklin chooses to believe that all booksellers share his love of books, even the cynics who 'cultivate a façade of indifference'. And while I could probably produce enough evidence to prove him wrong on that score, predominantly from among the men who pose as bibliophiles, it would not be necessary, because the assertion is substantiated by Franklin's personal bookselling code, which sets him apart from most of his contemporaries.

With few exceptions, Franklin buys only books he likes and would wish to possess. Ostensibly this classes him with the collector, except that he is professional enough to accept the inevitability of losing them in due course. Desirable or not, all books are purely regarded as stock, since every dealer must hold a stock unless he is merely a 'runner'.* In consequence, the argument among antiquarian booksellers over the merits of 'holding' rare items simply because they are irreplaceable becomes an irrelevance to him; one hangs on to or sells a book for reasons which should take no account of it being replaced. Why *should* we want to replace books? he enquires. Beautiful or very rare books are to be savoured and then simply passed on for the enjoyment of others.

What delights Franklin about bookselling is the freedom to do as he wishes, although even in his publishing days he produced books he considered ought to be put before the public rather because of their merits than because they would sell well. Essential to him is the freedom to not represent collectors or institutions at auctions, an occupation, to him, as boring as the routine of knowing everything there is to know about one's speciality while staying within the safe confines of that knowledge. This, after all, is a man who started as a specialist in private presses but found that too restricting and moved on to wider horizons, learning as he went. On a day when I called, he was excited by the novelty of having bought a collection of nineteenth-century French posters, about which he knew very little but which would give him pleasure until, perhaps much later, they appreciated in value sufficiently to re-sell. But a more dramatic illustration of faith in his own judgement—a self-assurance he defines as 'arrogance'—was the investment in works of members of the Designer Bookbinders when many of them were just beginning to find their feet, long before their individual talents were

---

* Someone who hurries from dealer to dealer, buying and selling at small margins for a quick turnover, often clinching sales before the books are actually in his possession.

universally acknowledged. Some of these brilliant artists and craftsmen consider Franklin to be an important benefactor of modern binding.

His entry into antiquarian bookselling in 1970 was financed by the sale of his almost complete personal collection of the Kelmscott Press titles printed on vellum (and so very rare) to the big-spending American dealer, L. D. Feldman. Franklin had already prepared his first private-presses catalogue from which, ironically, little else was sold at the time. From then on he concentrated on international book fairs, where most of his selling is done, frequently simply buying at one and selling at another. He takes a book only once, so that collectors and interested dealers know from experience that anything on the stand is 'fresh'. He prefers to let people discover something new than to tempt comments like 'Wasn't that here last year?', or 'Wasn't that in your catalogue four years ago?'. He never, incidentally, catalogues incunabula or early manuscript material, partly for that reason, but also because he feels that catalogues provide a temptation to boost one's ego or reputation, to show off the 'wonderful' things one, as a bookseller, has managed to acquire. In fact, he has issued little more than one or two catalogues a year, and, despite the apparent contradiction, his 1977 *Early Colour Printing: from Chiaroscuro to Aquatint*, hardbound and illustrated in colour, was offered for sale at £15—although this publication, with essays and much original information, is more a work of reference than catalogue, since it covers only nine items or collections (ranging in price from $1,250 to $50,000). Only 500 copies were printed; 200 were issued in a bid to attract the few potential customers and the rest were offered for sale. A target of nine buyers indicates Franklin's preference for fewer and fewer, that is better and better, books as opposed to large collections; his method is thus worlds apart from something like the Booth operation.

So, having covered both ends of the spectrum, who could have escaped the net? You may have gathered from the mixed bag I have presented that, in my opinion, formal recognition by the parent authority is seldom in itself a guideline to greatness. In all walks of life there are 'political' animals—the 'joiners'—and those who prefer to stay in the shadow. And, obviously, for every worthy President of the Antiquarian Booksellers' Association, there are half a dozen men or women of equal distinction. Similarly, there are those who are repeatedly singled out for public recognition, one honour attracting a second, while fellow members of the trade of perhaps greater industry, acumen or knowledge are overlooked. When the Association was founded in 1906, Henry N. Stevens, a specialist in Americana, became its first president, and was most probably an excellent choice. Stevens attracted honours; to be fair, without seeking them. But in 1923 on his last visit to the United States, he was awarded an honorary MA by the University of Michigan, and, when he died seven years later, the British Museum took the unprecedented step of paying an official tribute to his efforts in supplying them with Americana.

Yet, although there can be little dispute over the qualifications of H. N. Stevens, he was not necessarily any better equipped than his father, Henry, who came to England in the 1840s from Vermont, or his uncle Benjamin Franklin Stevens, who had joined his older brother a few years later. Neither received any honour in his lifetime, but the brothers must have been among the first bookseller-scholars, transcribing and issuing facsimiles of manuscripts in Europe relating to American history; for example, Henry's *Recollections of Mr James and the Founding of his Library*.

Benjamin Franklin Stevens, founder of B. F. Stevens & Brown Ltd, was probably the more interesting of the two, being a dynamic businessman also. Having started his own firm in 1864, he was officially appointed American Despatch Agent in London —the office responsible for receiving and forwarding all State Department and Army and Navy correspondence, a kind of Consulate and American Express benevolent authority in one. Needless to say, this work brought him into contact with some of the most interesting and important US citizens, and he dealt not only in books and art but with almost all related problems until the end of the century.

So, with respect to many fine Association Presidents over the years, I have chosen to evaluate achievements exclusively in *bookselling*. My selection of men who set standards as well as trends is in no way complete; indeed, in any 'best' list there are always controversial omissions. It does, however, at least provide a yardstick against which one can measure incidents and highlights in the story yet to be unfolded.

3 The Literary Detective

There is, of course, no substitute for luck when it is available on tap. The trouble is, luck is not the most predictable of the gifts bestowed upon us, and one really needs to fall back on something more dependable, like hard work. The dividing-line between scholarship and unspectacular, down-to-earth powers of detection is a fine one, and a bookseller or collector needs a combination of both. Persistence, a quality common to both, is essential in efforts to track down or identify the rare item, because sudden mind-boggling flashes of inspiration occur rarely, except in fiction. I am reminded of a Paul Gallico short story, *The Roman Kid*, in which a sports writer is able through Holmes-like powers of deduction, when professors of history and archaeology are baffled, to put a name to an unidentified statue of a Roman athlete simply because of his technical knowledge of boxing.

With books such inspiration is seldom necessary since information is usually available if one knows where to look for it—which is where the expertise comes in. Luck, as I said earlier, can play an important part, and sometimes fate alone hands the quest to us on a plate; but more often than not specialist knowledge of one sort or another is needed. It was luck that brought the Carolina Charter to the shop of Charles Traylen (bad luck, perhaps, which prevented him from finding it in the first place), but it was his initial hunch sparked by a degree of knowledge, and subsequent research, that identified the scroll for what it was.

People do sometimes literally stumble across 'treasures'. Some years ago, Sam Dauber, of Dauber & Pine, the Manhattan book firm, knocked over a pile of pamphlets which had been gathering dust for years. The odd one that caught his eye as he picked them up was Edgar Allan's Poe's *Murders in the Rue Morgue*, an offprint from a magazine made up as a salesman's sample in an edition of fifty to sixty. The discovery represents probably only four or five copies still in existence. This copy was quickly sold for $25,000. When I checked the story, the firm seemed embarrassed, as though introducing the element of luck was somehow a reflection on their professional skills. There is, unfortunately, a vein of snobbishness running through certain booksellers which compels them to maintain the mystique of unfathomed depths of knowledge, exclusive to their profession (note, not 'trade' on these occasions). Dealers who put on such airs might do well to remember their stallholder antecedents!

There has always been an element of social or intellectual snobbery in the book world, dating back perhaps to the early days of printing. Certainly, in the latter half of the fifteenth century, the presses were kept running only by the nobility's appetite for translations and abridgements of the classics and for foreign literature. Caxton, speaking of his *Boke of Eneydos*, says: 'This present book is not for a rude uplandish man to labour therein, nor read it: but only for a clerk and a noble gentleman, that feeleth and understandeth in feats of arms, in love, and in noble chivalry.' But then Caxton did not have to worry about upsetting the public at large; he had a very limited target audience.

Before I ramble off along another side avenue, I should really define 'scholarship'; at least, differentiate between the bookseller who has done his home-work, and is therefore an apparent mine of knowledge, and the 'pure' bibliographer. The librarian and researcher who spend their lives sorting out what most of us would regard as unimportant details are experts who are not terribly concerned with the value or literary content of the books and manuscripts placed under their magnifying glass; they are concerned more with tying an identity tag to each title, no matter how many editions it carried.

Probably the most striking example of bibliographical expertise is *A Short-Title Catalogue of Books Printed in England, Scotland and Ireland and of English Books Printed Abroad 1475–1640*, originally compiled by A. W. Pollard and G. R. Redgrave, of the British Museum, and published in 1926. Since this is a book to which many readers over the years ahead will wish to refer, in identifying and locating early printed material, it is worth elaborating on those dates. The opening date, of course, refers to the year in which Caxton set up his printing press in London; 1640 was fixed as the closing date because it was a demarcation line, signalling an end to the power of the Star Chamber a year later. Fear of the real and imagined influence of the press is not the prerogative of twentieth-century governments, and the Elizabethan and Stuart periods saw printers kept on a very tight rein (a decree of the Star Chamber in 1637 limited the number of type founders in England to four).

The STC (short-title catalogue) inspired Donald Wing of Yale University Library to compile something similar for the richer years from 1641 to 1700 (including titles from British America); it was published in four volumes between 1945 and 1955 and is a highly respected work, known simply as Wing. A catalogue of the period from 1701 to 1800, which will include more than half a million titles, is in the planning stage, and will probably not be published before the early 1980s.

In 1946, the Bibliographical Society decided to revise the first catalogue. Several learned and highly industrious bibliographers have worked on the revisions entailed in producing a 'new' STC issued in alphabetical instalments. Volume 2 (I–Z) was finally issued in 1977; Volume 1 is scheduled for 1980; and a final volume including a printers' index for two years later. The catalogue not only charts every early printed book that has been traced, but also details of very complex publications, such as the *Book of Common Prayer*, with its umpteen editions. It also lists, for every title, up to five separate locations on each side of the Atlantic, chosen with a wide geographical spread to make life easier for visiting scholars who wish to consult the originals. It is no exaggeration to say that researchers like Katherine F. Pantzer (who completed Volume 2), of Harvard's Houghton library, who devote their lives to the cause of literary scholarship, not only need memories like computers, but the stamina of a shirehorse.

In general, however, specialists who work on a reference book of such importance are more likely to spend their time sifting through mountains of corroborative evidence, requested and supplied by other bibliographers at the various international sources of information, with little time left to actually hit the treasure trail in the search for 'lost' masterpieces. Obviously, few of us set off each day with the express object of finding a long-lost piece of incunabula; nevertheless it still remains the dream of most booksellers and collectors. But where to search? The last place one would choose to look for an unusual tree would be in a forest, yet on several occasions rare volumes and manuscripts have turned up in a library. They remain undetected, sometimes because the librarian dealing with them is new, and is not really sure what he has in his possession, and sometimes simply because the 'treasure' has never been isolated from the wealth of material all around. After all, books do tend to look alike! Blackwell's of Oxford once managed to acquire one of only two known copies of the Pickering edition of William Dunbar poems, printed on vellum; the announcement was hailed with excitement by a well known Scottish library who agreed to buy the copy, only to cancel the order a few days later when it was discovered that they already owned the only other copy!

In 1976, a Belfast schoolmaster, Colin McKelvie identified in a public library in Northern Ireland something unique—a first edition of *Gulliver's Travels*, 1726, with extensive changes made by Swift in his own handwriting. However, this time I am not referring to a dusty old volume retrieved from a cobwebbed corner. The authorities were fully aware of this book and its literary significance, but no one had believed them! The library is no ordinary local library: it belongs to the Anglican cathedral of Armagh and, according to McKelvie, a student of eighteenth-century (and especially Irish) literature, it is full of literary treasures. But, presumably because it is not situated in London or one of the accepted centres of learning, no one had ever bothered to see for themselves. Indeed, earlier suggestions that the book—in the library since 1860—had been annotated by Swift were promptly dismissed by the so-called experts, including one leading US authority who had not actually seen it. McKelvie, who had studied the book for many hours and, as a student of Swift, had satisfied himself, could not understand why no one would listen. He obtained permission to take photostats, and sent copies to London, to David Woolley, a historian and a specialist on Swift and the period. McKelvie's suspicions were at last confirmed and the critics finally had to eat humble pie.

The changes in the printed text are fascinating: they were made by the printer Benjamin Motte who got cold feet at Swift's oblique reference to politicians and the establishment in thinly disguised satire, and who applied his own form of censorship. Subsequently Swift went through the book, page by page, marking changes he required in a text that had been 'basely mangled and abused', added to, and blotted out by the printer. Among the seventy-five specific items Motte had modified was a reference to the Emperor offering silk threads of purple, yellow and white (instead of red, blue and green) to those courtiers most accomplished in leaping and creeping, because Swift's colours were those of the order of the Thistle, Bath and the Garter. Five whole paragraphs, recognisable as a parody of the British plan to debase the Irish currency in 1724, were deleted by Motte. A passage ridiculing the legal profession was also cut out. In common with many writers, I have over the years endured the well meaning efforts of printers in 'correcting' or endeavouring to improve my spelling and grammar, but deletions are a bit much! And Motte was also inconsistent, objecting to Swift's strong views, but not afraid to introduce a few of his own, such as an implication that Queen Anne was a despot because she governed without a first minister—this disgusted Swift, who supported Anne, as opposed to George I and the Whigs. There was also another contradiction: in a list of vices which Swift said would disappear from the court if the lifestyle of the fictitious Houyhnhnms were adopted 'whoring' was included and left by Motte. For some reason Swift then deleted this word himself.

Swift died in 1745, and the marked book was included when his library was sold, although how it came to be in the Armagh library no one knows. One side-benefit of the 'discovery' is that the true 'original' version of *Gulliver's Travels* was later published to mark the 250th anniversary of the first edition.

If a library makes an excellent hiding place, books themselves are even more effective, provided the hidden item is small enough.

B. F. Stevens & Brown, international booksellers with a long history, made one of their most interesting purchases through an English doctor holidaying in Kent. While the eagle-eyed doctor was browsing through a small private library he encountered an old volume of sermons and tracts, and inside found something most unexpected, *The Laws of Massachusetts* (first edition, 1648). Being the smallest tract in the volume, it escaped damage when the binder trimmed the edges, and was therefore in its original uncut state. The find is now in the Huntington library.

The same firm had a similar piece of good fortune when it obtained another seventeenth-century treasure, although this time it came as a reward for some diligent detective work in another area. In its earlier days, Stevens & Brown dealt in fine art as well as books, and before World War I Ralph Brown was asked to trace a portrait of Sir Edmund Andros (1637–1714), Colonial Governor of New York, New England and Virginia. The only information provided was that there *had* been a portrait at some time, and that it had been in the possession of the Andros family 'somewhere in England'. Since the family's fortunes had declined in the ensuing two hundred years, the task initially proved insurmountable. But Brown refused to concede defeat. Whenever travelling to different parts of the country, something he did automatically was to check the local directories, and eventually he found a ray of hope, an anonymous sounding Mr Andros in Surrey. With fingers crossed, he called on Mr Andros and found himself face-to-face with the last in the family line, and, in the hallway, the portrait of Sir Edmund. For the time being, Brown had to settle for a photograph as proof of the portrait's existence, but when Mr Andros eventually decided to sell, he was able to find a private buyer who presented it to Harvard. The reward, to which I referred, followed. Having established a rapport, Mr Andros then presented him with a cardboard box full of oddments which the gentleman thought 'might be of some interest'. The first 'oddment' removed from the box proved to be Charles II's Royal Warrant authorising 'our cousin', Sir Edmund Andros, to take over from the Dutch the city of New Amsterdam, henceforth to be known as New York. The Warrant was later presented to the New York Historical Association. It might be said that some people make their own luck.

George Friderick Handel the composer (1685–1759) also qualifies for this chapter because, like Swift, he was 'lost' in a library. (There is another reason for mentioning him: he was probably the first composer to merit a biography, and a few years ago a copy of the 1760 first edition was found with annotations in the hand of Charles Jennens, Handel's friend who compiled the libretto for the *Messiah*.)

Handel's music for *Comus*, assumed to have been lost after a private performance in 1748, was found in 1967 in Manchester Central Library (where, incidentally, some hitherto unknown Vivaldi sonatas were also discovered). The discovery was made by music critic Anthony Hicks, who paid a visit to the Henry Watson Music Library (part of the Central Library) when he heard that Sir Newman Flower's collection of music—mainly Handel and other eighteenth-century composers—which also included the associated Aylesford collection, had not been examined in detail, and therefore offered interesting possibilities. The collection was accompanied by a duplicated list, but some of the titles and names meant very little. *Comus*, based on Milton's poem (in fact, written in 1634 and intended as a masque on the theme of maidenly purity) was twice played and performed by bass and soprano voices, at a private party for the Earl of Gainsborough, in 1745 and 1748. The music, apparently, was then lost. Hicks had nothing special in mind as he browsed through the collection, until he came to some music called *Serenata*; but, although he was intrigued by it, all he could do at that stage was to copy down the beginning of each of the pieces. Later he noticed similar music in Handel's oratorio, the *Occasional*, and came to the conclusion that the *Comus* material had been adapted and used for this six months later. Two years elapsed before Hicks was satisfied that his hunch had been correct. He was re-reading an article when certain information hitherto overlooked suddenly stood out as relative to his quest—letters written to the Fourth Earl of Shaftesbury, two of which actually referred to pieces produced by Handel for the *Comus* recital. The description of the music was identical with that found by Hicks, although why his discovery was entitled

Serenata is not explained (although it is in the hand of a copyist, and not Charles Jennens as might have been supposed). He then found that the lyrics were adapted from the epilogue to Milton's work. Musicologists consider the *Comus* music to be representative of Handel at his best and, as a belated celebration of the find, the pieces were performed at Birmingham University in 1977, just 229 years after the previous concert.

There is a danger of over-dramatizing 'finds' and the detective work involved. Lesson one is never to assume that a 'rare' book is unavailable, and to begin from the beginning. Only a few years ago I was hunting for a very scarce Samuel Pepys item, the two-volume *Occasional Papers Published for Members of the Samuel Pepys Club.** The publication was limited to 250 copies and, as any Pepys collector will tell you, these are very scarce and in great demand. After further enquiries in the trade, I happened to be at George Bell & Son, the publishers who have produced much other Pepys material, including the latest edition of the *Diaries*, and grumbled to a veteran warehouseman about the disappearance of the *Occasional Papers*. After a moment's sympathetic reflection, he excused himself, returning five minutes later, somewhat dusty, from the furthermost depths of the basement. In his hand were two volumes, new, and in their original plain paper dust wrappers. 'I thought I remembered seeing some old books around,' he said, identifying the *Occasional Papers*. For the price, he referred to the oldest Bell catalogue he could find, and I left a few moments later delighted at the price—about 30s (£1.50), an incredible bargain. The irony, as any bookseller will confirm, is that all too often when one orders a new book from the publisher, only a few months after publication, one is told 'sorry—out-of-print'. *Occasional Papers* may have been reported out-of-print forty odd years earlier, but for some reason there was still one copy left in the least likely place.

Unlike the modern policeman, the bibliophile taking on the rôle of detective faces an enormous handicap because in most cases

---

* Ed. Philip Norman, Vol. I 1903–14, printed by The Chiswick Press, 1917, and Vol. II 1917–23, published 1927.

the 'witnesses' to the disappearance of the books he seeks are dead or have themselves disappeared. Tracking down a whole collection might be easier, one would imagine, than tracking down a single volume, but again there is no hard and fast rule. One of the most fascinating searches ever undertaken, and one in which you, the reader, are invited to participate, is for an almost complete parish library (in fact, three libraries) which disappeared about seventy years ago, probably to the personal gain of a little known country parson, a real-life character who might have stepped out of the pages of a Sherlock Holmes short story.

The driving force behind the search, which has gradually gathered momentum since the early 1960s, is Canon John A. Fitch, Vicar at Brandon in Suffolk, UK, and Chairman of St Edmondsbury and Ipswich Diocesan Parochial Libraries Committee. Canon Fitch has worked in Suffolk for thirty years since taking a degree in history at Cambridge, and, although always a bibliophile, he was barely aware of the existence of parochial libraries until we went to an exhibition of church treasures in 1961. Indeed, one of the frustrations of the antiquarian-book world is the constant awareness of one's ignorance of areas outside one's immediate interest, although all we can do is accept our limitations and hope to learn something every day. For example, I did not know, until Canon Fitch drew my attention to the fact, that in 1959, following the increasing number of sales of old church libraries, Doctor Geoffrey Fisher, then Archbishop of Canterbury, set up a high-powered committee of bookmen to report on the overall situation in England and Wales.

The interest and enthusiasm stimulated by their activity fired John Fitch who began by cataloguing the Beccles Parish Library, and then joined the Parochial Libraries committee of which he was to become chairman. The situation with which he became acquainted was that, until 1890, there had been, in the various churches and parsonages in Suffolk, eleven parochial libraries, founded between 1590 and 1790. Since then, three of these had simply disappeared. The library already mentioned, and the most interesting, was that of Brent Eleigh, a beautiful village of under two hundred people, just two miles from Lavenham. The others were Milden, an adjoining parish (now combined with two others in one benefice) and Sudbury All Saints, the smallest, which had only sixty-two volumes at the outset.

It was obviously impractical to expect that any of the missing books could ever be returned, since they had presumably been purchased in good faith, but the committee was determined to trace their movements and discover their final resting place, if nothing else. With the help of friends such as Michael Tupling, librarian at the County Library at Bury St Edmunds, John Fitch began his search, directing his attention principally at libraries and booksellers through professional and trade journals on both sides of the Atlantic. Letters projecting the background to the three libraries appeared in such journals as *The Book Collector*, *The Papers of the Bibliographical Society of America*, *Notes and Queries*, *The Bibliothek* (Scottish journal of bibliography) and the Library Association's *Rare Books Group Newsletter*.

Before moving on to the results of his early efforts, let me give you an outline description of the libraries and books which have caused so much trouble:

Sudbury All Saints was relatively insignificant, notable only as an example of the libraries set up and sent out by Doctor Thomas Bray and his friends. (Doctor Bray was the divine and philanthropist who did so much to inspire the public-library movement in England and America in the late seventeenth and early eighteenth centuries.) Dating from 1712, the library, judging from a surviving list, comprised only standard works of divinity.

The *Milden* library of over two hundred volumes was left by William Burkitt, Rector of Milden (d. 1703)—and vicar and lecturer of Dedham, Essex—who is remembered by New Testament scholars for his *Expository Notes*, reprinted many times in the eighteenth century. In accordance with the terms of his will, the library remained at Milden Rectory until 1904 when the rector of that time, the Reverend A. F. Rivers, sent it to the Sudbury Archdeaconery Bray Library at Bury St Edmunds, with a recommendation that the old books be sold and replaced with modern theology more 'useful' to the twentieth-century clergyman! (Where have we heard that story before?) The efforts of Rivers' successor to obtain the books' return were blocked, and suddenly the Burkitt books disappeared *en masse*. One volume was reported seen in a Charing Cross Road bookshop some years ago, but was sold again before it could be recovered. To complicate the issue, there is no known catalogue.

The more intriguing *Brent Eleigh* library was founded by the will of Henry Colman, DD, Fellow of Trinity College, Cambridge, Rector of Harpley, Norfolk, and Squire (but not Rector) of Brent Eleigh, who died in 1715. 'My Library of Books ... I leave altogether and dedicate and consecrate to the use of the Church of Brentily [sic] that is the incumbent Minister there for ever subject to the order of the [1709] Act of Parliament in that case provided.' The books were housed in a purpose-built brick library adjoining the church, and remained there until 1859 when the library was pulled down and replaced by a separate building in the churchyard. The £1,000 bond of 1720 signed by the then rector, Thurloe, and binding him and his successors to maintain the library inviolate, according to the terms of Colman's will, survives in the Norfolk and Norwich Record Office, and attached to it is a complete catalogue, closely written on two large parchments, of the 1,700 or so volumes. Besides a fifteenth-century manuscript of Martial's *Epigrams*, the library included a wide collection of Divinity—particularly strong in the Greek and Latin Fathers—together with classics, English and European history, some law books, a few atlases, and a considerable amount of contemporary religious, political and academic polemical writing (including Swift's *Tale of a Tub*, 1704). Other medieval manuscripts were added about 1727.

The then rector and churchwarden sold the manuscripts (but not the books) at Sotheby's in 1887 and 1891, and all survive. They include Saint Margaret of Scotland's *Gospels*, sold to the Bodleian in 1887 for £6. *The Martial* was sold to Cambridge University Library for £16, and four years later other manuscripts were acquired by the University Library and the Fitzwilliam Museum, including a *Life* of Saint William of Norwich. The printed books, however, disappeared without trace some time after 1891.

Considering the wide circulation of the journals to which John Fitch wrote, the results of the book search have been disappointing, although each new piece of evidence has obviously opened up

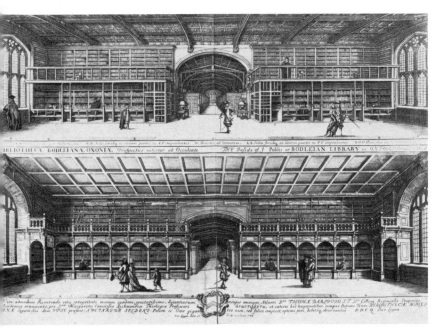

The Bodleian Library, Oxford, from David Loggan, *Oxonia illustrata*, 1675. The top plate is of Art's End, the lower of Selden End. (*Courtesy of the Bodleian Library*)

Eighteenth-century oil painting on wood, depicting the interior of an Italian bookshop—identified as that of Tumermani of Verona, who was a seller of both new and antiquarian books, better known as a publisher.

The plaques on the wall show works published by Tumermani and the portraits are probably of Turmani's authors. (*Courtesy of Thomas Cook, The College Gateway Bookshop, Ipswich*)

The chest of Reverend Scrope Davies, opened after 150 years to reveal original manuscripts of Byron and Shelley. (*Courtesy of Barclays Bank Ltd*)

'Traditional' fine binding for Whistler's *The Gentle Art of Making Enemies*, 1890 Designed and bound by Sangorski and Sutcliffe, who originated the peacock binding style, in crushed levant morocco, tooled in gilt, with an inlaid miniature ruby eye, and variations of Whistler's butterfly monogram at each corner and on the spine. (*Courtesy of Charles J. Sawyer*)

another avenue of enquiry. For example, in all these years only one item from the Milden collection has been identified, and this was unearthed by John Lancaster, at the Houghton Library of Harvard University. It was a collection of tracts and pamphlets by Thomas Shepherd (1605–49), one of the founders of the University. After seeing a reference to Milden in the *Papers of the Bibliographical Society of America*, Lancaster checked and found reference to it in the provenance catalogue. The outcome was the discovery of the Milden Library inscription behind the bookplate 'Harvard College Library 1916', the book having been from the collection of Frederick Lewis Gay. However, Lancaster's catalogue covers only books processed since the Houghton library was opened in 1943, and the half million volumes housed there but not so far processed, in addition to volumes in the Andover Harvard Divinity library, may well contain 'strays' from Suffolk. The proper processing of vast library stocks is not an uncommon problem, and, with the numbers involved, it is not surprising that Harvard's reaction was that there was 'no way' of finding other possible Milden material for the present.

The Brent Eleigh search has been more productive, although also disappointing: only six volumes have so far been found. One, Samuel Newman's *A Concordance of the Holy Scriptures* (Cambridge, 1698), also turned up in the United States, at the Folger Shakespeare Library, in Washington. The reference librarian there sent John a photocopy of Henry Colman's autograph and the manuscript press marks from the inner front cover. This folio volume was bought by Folger from Bernard Quaritch (catalogue 361, 1921) but the invoice still recorded does not indicate other purchases at the same time. Naturally the Quaritch clue was followed up, but their records produced another dead end.

In 1968 *Oratores veteres* (Paris, 1575) was found in Uraban University Library, Illinois, by which it had been purchased in 1949. Inside was a handwritten 'Brent Ely [sic] Library' bookplate with class marks, identical with that in the Cambridge University library Epigrams. In 1976, the same bookplate was found in a second edition of Samuel Woodford's *Paraphrase of the Psalms of David* (London, 1678) at the University of Glasgow to which it has been donated in 1919 by the Very Reverend James Cooper, then Professor of Ecclesiastical History, and sometime Moderator of the Church of Scotland. How it came into the possession of Reverend Cooper is not known.

Two other items from the library turned up in the collection of an antiquarian bookseller, G. V. M. Heap of Wells, Somerset, whose interest was aroused by Canon Fitch's letter in *The Library*. Heap, apart from offering various constructive suggestions for follow-up enquiries, remembered where he had purchased one volume (at a bookshop in Devon). He also recalled being conscious at the time of its Brent Eleigh marking; but, yet again, the investigations came to nothing.

In 1977, the sixth item turned up in unexpected place: it was found by a librarian among the Brent Eleigh manuscripts at the University library, Cambridge. The librarian had been working on a catalogue of medieval manuscripts and had traced some of them back to Lord William Howard of Carlisle, an enthusiastic book collector at the time of Elisabeth I and James I. With the manuscript, acquired at the auction of 1891 largely through the efforts of Montague James, Provost of Kings College, was just *one* book from Brent Eleigh: William Rastell's *A Table Collected of the Yeres* [sic] *of Our Lord God and The Years of the Kings of England* (London, 1571). Inside was the 1727 signature of a clergyman, Fane Edge, a descendant of the Fane family, Earls of Westmoreland, indicating a connection with the Howards.

Other investigations, more intensive than the essentially long-term communication with librarians and booksellers, have been made through a more direct line of enquiry in the village itself and in surrounding areas—people with long memories have been questioned, the local records searched, and the descendants and relatives of all the rectors since 1890 have been contacted. Diocesan records reveal that no rectors disappeared in suspicious circumstances; nor was there any report of uncharacteristically lavish church expenditure. One can only conclude that the library was sold by someone for personal profit. If the books had been stolen in the normal way then the rector of the time would presumably have reported the incident, so the finger of suspicion points to one of the incumbents. Highly discreet cloak-and-dagger investigations have narrowed the list of suspects to one man who, unfortunately, cannot be identified here, since he has living relatives. The evidence is in any case highly circumstantial.

Indeed, I wonder whether the innocent, even 'holier-than-thou', images of many of those investigated and 'discarded' by our intrepid detectives could not have concealed a fiendishly cunning book thief. Our prime suspect was instantly damned by his reputation: a secret opium smoker (how Holmes would love to have met him!) and a brandisher of knives in frequent skirmishes with his wife, his name not surprisingly crops up as the suspect in any strange incident in Suffolk—even those dating back years before he was even born! You and I know, of course, that book thieves are invariably 'respectable' figures, which would have immediately disqualified him in my eyes, but Canon Fitch and his friends have stoically kept an open mind—and still come to a dead end.

So, if you have any ideas, or wish to help in some way, I am sure any contribution would be welcomed by John Fitch and his committee, who expect the search to continue probably into the next century. Further local information on the subject can be found in an introduction the Canon has written for *Suffolk Parochial Libraries: A Catalogue*, published at the end of 1977.

Our Brent Eleigh drug addict was in no way unique; there is no doubt that the mantle of divinity has cloaked the baser inclinations of many a hell-raider. One such fascinating character, the Reverend Scrope Berdmore Davies (1782–1852), was indirectly responsible for what in 1976 was described as the literary find of the century: original and hitherto unknown manuscripts of Byron and Shelley, thought to be worth between £250,000 and £500,000! The material, deposited by Davies in a locked chest in 1820 before he fled to France to escape his creditors, included: Byron's manuscript of the Third Canto of *Childe Harold's Pilgrimage*, written in the poet's own handwriting in a red leather notebook; a fair copy of *The Prisoner of Chillon*, with amendments in his writing; and a notebook in Shelley's handwriting, containing his manuscript of the *Hymn to Intellectual Beauty*, together with what appeared to be two new poems. Correspondence from the poets and other members of their circle—Thomas Moore, Augusta Leigh (Byron's half-sister), Lady Caroline Lamb, John Cam Hobhouse and Charles Skinner Matthews—throws new light on Byron's life and reveals Davies as one of the poet's closest friends and confidants.

The chest was opened, more than 150 years after being deposited by Davies, only because the West End branch of Barclay's Bank, where it was housed, was due for alterations. In the course of the upheaval 'old' deposits were looked at for the first time in many years, and, where no ownership was apparent, the boxes were opened and their contents examined.

Let us start by trying to picture Scrope Davies, about which little had been known, by using this extract from *Alumni Cantabrigienses:*

> . . . admitted King's Coll, Camb, as a scholar (from Eton) 8 July 1802; BA 1806; MA 1809; Fellow 1809 to his death; Eton Coll. Betham Scholar, 1803–1816; remarkable for his dexterity at all athletic games; intimate friend of Tom Moore and of Lord Byron (who dedicated *Parisina* to him, and who, from his death bed, sent him a ring); one of the most distinguished wits in London at the time of the Regency; lived in Ostend 1836 and latterly in Paris, where he d.23 or 24 May 1852 . . .

The saga of the chest begins in 1816 when the Shelleys—Percy Bysshe, his wife Mary and her step-sister Claire Clairmont—spent a holiday on the shores of Lake Geneva with Lord Byron. Byron is said to have conducted a casual love affair with Claire, and allowed her to make copies of the poem he wrote. In August, Davies, accompanied by John Cam Hobhouse, arrived for a short visit to Byron. A few days later Shelley had to return to England, and, to ensure the safe delivery of his new poems, Byron gave copies to Shelley and his recently arrived friend. To Shelley he gave the *Childe Harold* transcript in Claire's writing and to Davies the copy in his own hand. Indeed, to Claire's version he added a note: 'This copy is to be printed from—subject to comparison with the original manuscript (from which this is a transcription) in such parts as it may chance to be difficult to decipher in the following.' We owe our knowledge of the poem to Shelley—for the Scrope Davies 'authentic' version just disappeared.

Imagine being handed an original masterpiece for publication and simply forgetting all about it. There is no sensible reason why the manuscript should still have been in the possession of Davies four years later, when he dumped his treasures and fled to France. Shelley, it seems, had also been too trusting, yet there was something about Davies which held their friendship. Byron, in fact, later shrugged off this unreliability as the result of 'an inaccurate memory'.

Apart from one short visit to London in disguise, Scrope Davies remained abroad, dying in poverty and exile. The locked trunk was left unclaimed in the custody of his bankers, Morland Ransom & Company which, after various changes of name, became part of Barclay's Bank at the end of the nineteenth century. When the old bank buildings were pulled down the box was moved—unopened—and, as we have seen, it was not examined until 1976. Apart from the manuscripts already mentioned there were thirteen letters, dating from 1809 to 1819, from Byron to Scrope Davies, and such fascinating period ephemera as betting slips and promissory notes, and, equally interesting to historians, some original material relating to Napoleon. Davies' younger brother, Samuel, an officer in the Royal Navy, had been on board HMS Northumberland when she transported the Emperor to St Helena. As well as letters to his older brother, Samuel sent him sketches of Napoleon drawn on the voyage.

The documents, after being declared authentic, were handed over to the British Library, since legal ownership would be almost impossible to ascertain. Davies was one of ten children and the laws of Intestacy applying in 1852 provided that his personal estate should be divided between living brothers and sisters, and the various nephews and nieces. Owing to the number of generations that have passed in the ensuing 125 years, definitive ownership could be an insoluble problem, and members of the family who have been traced have approved of the indefinite arrangements with the British Library.

But, to return to detective work.

Alan G. Thomas has been a bookseller since 1927, dealing mainly in fine books, and has acquired a reputation for producing fascinating catalogues. Most of this interest is the result of his own enthusiasm for the books and the lengths to which he is prepared to go in researching their history—studying not only the books, their authors, printers and binders, but also the collectors through whose hands the books have passed. Much of this requires a combination of leg work and scholarly knowledge and application. For example, he once bought a very rare copy of *The Book of Hawking, Hunting and Heraldry* (The Book of St Albans, 1486), of which only seventeen copies survive, most of them imperfect. The book is a highly desirable collector's item because of its double appeal: it is interesting to both students of early printing and followers of field sports—being the first British book with colour printing, the first on a sporting subject, the first English printed armorial, and the first English book with popular rhymes.

Thomas had for many years been captivated by this book, which he regards as the 'black tulip' of English incunabula, comparing his pre-ownership memories with 'pressing your face against the museum glass, and dreaming about something you'll never own'. The first time it appeared at auction just after World War II he had only just left military hospital and was not equipped for this different kind of battle. The second time, when it appeared in the Walter Hutchinson collection in 1950, he was armed with an inheritance, but failed by one £50 bid (it reached £1,600). But, on the third occasion, at the sale of the books of the Polar explorer, Cherry-Garrard, he acquired it for £2,400. Certain leaves were missing but on most of the others was a considerable amount of what a few booksellers of my acquaintance would call 'scribble', annotations in a contemporary hand. For some reason no one had paid much attention to this writing but, as he studied it, Thomas began to suspect that he was looking at the copy actually owned by Wynkyn de Worde, the mysterious schoolmaster printer, about whom little is known except that he had once worked for Caxton as an editor and compositor. Moreover, Thomas also felt that the writing indicated it had been used by Wynkyn de Worde to prepare for a revised edition (to be printed in 1496).

It is fairly common for people to assume that 'old' writing must necessarily have been penned by the author or by someone equally illustrious (except for the person mentioned elsewhere who thought everything had been written by Francis Bacon if accompanied by a pointing finger), so Thomas was exceptionally cautious. He said nothing to anyone, and took the copy to a leading expert on incunabula, George Painter of the British Museum, who was able to transform the morass of clues into tangible evidence to prove the point. He demonstrated, for example, that it had been marked for 'casting off', with the final page endings indicated, points checked and confirmed with the 1496 edition. There were also a number of textual amendments. The spelling in the original, St Albans edition was somewhat 'provincial' for the 'modern' taste of the reader of ten years later, so words and style had been updated; for example, plurals no longer ended in *is*. Apart from its contribution to the sparse knowledge of de Worde and his printing activities, the evidence also revealed that this may well be the only printed (as opposed to manuscript) 'copy' for an English incunabulum to have survived. Another unique feature is that another copy owned by the British Museum, hitherto described as 'uncut' measures $11\frac{1}{2}$ by $8\frac{3}{8}$ inches (about 290×210mm) compared to this one's $12\frac{3}{16}$ by $8\frac{3}{4}$ inches (about 310×220mm). Owing to the extra depth of the lower margins, the manuscript signatures (ordinal latin numbers for each quire) have survived in this copy only.

The 'business' sequel to the story is ironic. The British Museum was interested in buying the book and, aware that 'public' funds are limited, Thomas agreed, if they could raise the money, to let them have it for £3,240. Meanwhile, it had been catalogued for £12,500, and a customer found. While Thomas still awaited a delayed decision from the Museum Trustees, his client, acquainted with the situation, promised: 'I won't stand in their way, but if they turn it down I'll definitely buy it for £12,500.' It eventually went to the British Museum, with Thomas, like booksellers before him, willingly sacrificing over £9,000! The consolation, of course, is that he can go and see it from time to time in its showcase.

Among the transatlantic school of scholar-booksellers of the post-war years are the very experienced American partners, Leona Rostenberg and Madeleine B. Stern, whose joint autobiography *Old & Rare: Thirty Years in the Book Business*, was published in 1974. Two whole chapters were devoted to the topic of bibliographical detection related to their own detective activities which they covered under the heading 'Holmes and Watson'. The examples given are fascinating, but I was amused to see in a kindly review of the book by another respected scholar, Clifford Maggs of Maggs Brothers, that even accepted conclusions are still occasionally open to challenge. Not being a scholar, I am happy to believe most of the statements of 'fact' I read, but Maggs took mild exception to a claim that a 1634 edition of *Poemata* in the possession of the partners had been bound for the French collector, Jacques Auguste de Thou. Maggs pointed out that de Thou had died in 1617, seventeen years before publication, and concluded that the copy had presumably been bound for his eldest son, François Auguste (beheaded 1642), who did not have his own library stamp. I am now waiting for another bookseller to pop up with new information that François, in fact, had an illegitimate brother, Jacques, who shared his father's library stamp, and that it was he who really ordered the binding!

Compared with establishing ownership, checking the authenticity of a book or manuscript is comparatively simple. Nicholas Poole-Wilson, of Quaritch, once bought a single sheet from Valerius Maximus, a 1472 example of Netherlands printing, from a dealer in old masters who let it go since, with two thirds of the page printed, he considered it was more 'book' than work of art. The printer originally intended to illustrate the book with woodcuts, but they were never executed, so it was published with blank spaces, with a few copies subsequently illustrated by hand. The beautiful sheet, with fine illumination, was obtained by Poole-Wilson for $5,000. Forgeries of incunabula are exceptionally difficult to produce, but Poole-Wilson nevertheless decided to check. Only five single sheets had ever been traced and, as two of them were at Harvard, he went to the University Library to make comparisons. Not only were they obviously from the same printer and artist but the histories of their previous ownership tallied.

Not every bookseller has the time or resources to do much in the way of research. Charles Lloyd of New York found a manuscript journal in an attic in 1976 and, on starting to read the contents, realised it had belonged to George Howard, a major in the United States Army who became a political figure of some significance. The folio of 400 pages is concerned principally with an account of the 1812 war with Mexico, and in its report of the death of General Daniel Pike differs from the version generally accepted. Although he had a reasonable idea of the historical importance of his find, Lloyd took the journal to Princetown University for authentication. (Adding to its value were the autographs of four separate Presidents, and Howard's commission signed by James Madison.) Although he could have got more at auction, Lloyd followed the university's suggestion of letting it go to the New York Historical Association. (Actually, it had also American Old West associations because the author had copied a great number of letters from the Kansan, Henry Levingworth, a colonel in the war and a famous frontiersman.)

Finally, here are three examples of the part played by luck, although in the first it required an element of knowledge and research to 'convert' a windfall into a worthwhile sale.

Many Londoners will remember the days when the Farringdon Road book market was a mecca for bibliophiles (there are still a couple of stalls there, but nothing like the good old days). When still in publishing, Colin Franklin was browsing one day at one of the stalls among a huge pile of prints. When it started to rain, the unprotected drawings began to get wet. Franklin's concern for anything old and aesthetically pleasing got the better of him and he bought the prints—just to save them from possible disintegration. At the office he put them next to a heater to dry out, and then into an exceptionally large middle drawer of his desk. When he left the firm, the desk, which had belonged to his father, went with him. But he did not bother to clear out the middle drawer until several years later. When the prints were 'rediscovered' and examined properly there were one or two clues which justified further enquiries. It transpired that they were, in fact, progress proofs (unfinished) of prints made by John Boydell for his

Shakespeare Gallery series. Boydell, a former Lord Mayor of London, was an eighteenth-century print publisher who managed to get the great artists of the period—men of the stature of Reynolds—to paint scenes from Shakespeare from which he would make engravings. Franklin managed to get a copy of the book for which the series was commissioned and catalogued it, with the loose prints, for several hundred pounds. They went to the Paul Mellon collection in the United States.

Ralph Shrimph, of Cranberry Bookworm, New Jersey, did not even bother to check his facts when he stumbled across a couple of 'old' books tossed out with the garbage in a local garage. He recognised them instantly as Benjamin Franklin imprints, and took them to Sotheby Parke Bernet in Manhattan, where Cicero's *Cato Major* (Philadelphia 1744) fetched $700 and the very rare *Some Account of Pennsylvania Hospital* (Philadelphia 1754–61), two volumes in one, sold for $1,600. This last book gives a fascinating account of the founding and early days of the first hospital in what was then an English colony, and where Franklin was actually a manager.

For our third example we look to Galloway and Porter, the old-established Cambridge booksellers, the sort of firm that manages to hold many of its customers for a lifetime. They recall one collector who had taught at a school in the town and who had in 1938 arranged for Harrods, in London, to store his books for the duration of the war. They filled thirty crates. For some reason he never reclaimed them and, on his death many years later, his will revealed that his money and possessions were to go to one of the colleges at the University. This obviously included his books, and Stephen Porter the third-generation Porter of the bookshop, was given the task of sorting them. Most of the books were 'good' academic volumes, but in one crate he found a beautiful two-volume set of Ackerman's *Oxford* (1814) worth £1,250! Finding and returning to circulation such exquisite or rare books, is a rewarding experience that transcends personal interest.

4 Anecdotes from the Book World

Intrepid bookseller 'Mr X' tried to conceal his disappointment at
the abysmally low standard of the books he had come to appraise;
the journey had been wasted. When offered a cup of tea, the pana-
cea to any crisis in England, he moved disconsolately into the
dining room where he was greeted offensively by a parrot occupy-
ing a cage in the corner. His own instinctively rude response was
swallowed when he noticed the cage was resting on a book. A
closer look, and his eyes popped: it was a Kelmscott Chaucer, the
William Morris masterpiece, often said to be the finest book
since the revival of printing, and even possibly going right back
to the Gutenberg Bible. 'There is *one* book I would like . . .' he
declared. Alas, it was not for sale, being the only book on which
the parrot's cage would fit snugly.

This story, which eventually ended happily, is supposed to be
true and to have happened in the 1950s in London's Notting Hill
Gate . . . and Cheltenham . . . and, ah well, let us just say that
there are three or four dealers of integrity who swear it happened
to them and them alone. I suppose there could be three or four
parrots around who could corroborate the story, but really more
to the point is the fact that a number of 'treasures' have been
found by accident, a point upon which I have already elaborated.
Meanwhile, it should be understood that bookselling is one industry where an assistant does not have to be faced with demands
of 'sales, not tales', since tales are very much a part of the enchant-
ment of the business; perhaps even a strong selling feature in
their own right.

In certain trades and industries the energy generated by competitiveness and a general fascination for the 'product' spark off an undercurrent of excitement, an atmosphere in which interesting things just happen. Bookselling, unlike, say, the newspaper business, has retained much of that atmosphere and, while there might not be as many genuine 'characters' around today (are there in any walk of life?), there seems to be no end to the number of stories that continue to emerge. For example, Joseph's in London's Charing Cross Road, attracts bizarre stories in the same way as its busy corner site acts as a magnet for book thieves.

The Joseph family's involvement in books dates back to the 1780s, possibly earlier, although the shop did not trade under its present name until 1902. With browsers, and thieves, in mind, the outside of the shop is today covered with shelves of cheap books —one painless way of clearing unwanted stock. This was not always so, and one of the many anecdotes associated with the first Mr Joseph (they used to say 'Old Jo' but since his son, Sam Joseph, is a respected and active member of the trade now in his eighties, I would rather not confuse the issue) concerns perfectly good books that had been displayed on those shelves. The lower shelves frequently received the attentions, not of book thieves— presumably too lazy to stoop to that level—but of man's best friend. The books in question were twenty-one large volumes of Simeon's *Skeletons of Sermons*, sold to a country clergyman. They were in reasonable condition but for a strange smell rather different to the recognised odour of most old books. Old books do have a distinctive smell which most of us enjoy, but this was different. The customer bought them happily enough, but when he became increasingly aware of the odour he returned to complain. Apparently he had no answer to Mr Joseph's innocent explanation: 'My dear sir, I assumed you *wanted* an authority on dogmatic theology?'

Clergymen, as I suggested in the previous chapter, seem to be practically an integral part of booksellers' anecdotes. Peter Fenemore, manager of Blackwell's antiquarian-book department, recalls a visit during one bitterly cold winter to an old vicarage in

Manchester where there were many thousands of books for sale, all covered in layers of soot; how this had occurred was never explained. The chimneys had obviously not been swept for many years, and so there was no heating either; but, since the books were undoubtedly worth closer examination, a half-frozen Fenemore diligently ploughed through them with a colleague, both finishing like rejects from an audition for the Black and White Minstrel Show. Solicitously invited by the vicar to take a bath, they shivered their way to the bathroom where they found further virgin layers of soot. Nearly an hour was spent cleaning the bath before they could make themselves presentable—with cold water. I suppose, with all due respect to Blackwell's, it may not have been an anecdote to J. N. Bartfield who, if legend is correct, surely would have asked, '*What* soot?'

Blackwell's is, understandably, a highly respected business and, although the sale of antiquarian books represents only a small proportion of the company's £26 million turnover on books, it is itself a large and efficient operation with an international customer listing of thousands. Like Howes of Hastings, Blackwell's tends to specialise in scholarly books rather than in the vastly expensive rare works. But the limitations of their business horizons are part of a deliberate market policy, and, with the financial muscle of the Blackwell's organisation behind them, it would not be surprising to see them emerge as a major world force in the pure rare-books field. Success in business is not just a matter of money —football clubs have demonstrated that there is more to building a championship side than buying star players—but, when un-limited funds are poured into an already efficient operation, then watch out! Competition in the major antiquarian-book league does require big money and hence the financial backing of firms like Quaritch and Southeran; but, when a successful company is able to reinvest profits (which would otherwise be taxed) in stock that can only appreciate over the years, it has a tremendous advantage if helped by the knowledge and expertise of men like Fenemore and his colleagues.

Blackwell's has been commemorated in print. John Masefield wrote of them:

There, in the Broad, within whose booky house
Half England's scholars nibble books or browse;
Where'd they wander blessed fortune theirs . . .

The business was founded by Benjamin Henry Blackwell in 1879 with £150 lent by an enthusiastic customer. The earliest ledger shows that, in November of that year, a Doctor Jowett, Master of Balliol bought *Diodorus Siculus*, translated by Cogan, folio, for 7s 6d (37½p), which he paid in March 1881. But giving credit seems to have paid off, because the business prospered and today dominates Oxford. Just one of its bookrooms, built in 1966 under the neighbouring Trinity College, has earned a place in *The Guiness Book of Records* as constituting the largest display of books anywhere in the world in a single room (160,000 volumes on two and a half miles of shelving).

Some of the more interesting stories in the antiquarian world have less to do with a dealer's experience than with the book itself. Even the dispassionate investor cannot fail to be stirred by some of the circumstances in which books ultimately arrive on the market. Who would not give his eye teeth for a certain little green morocco volume from the collection of Marie Antoinette? Kept by her side until the moment of her execution, the book, with the coat of arms removed from the cover, *Office de la Divine Providence* (Paris 1757), has these notes written on the flyleaf: '*Ce 16 Octobre, a 4 h.½ du matin. Mon Dieu! ayez pitie de moi! Mes yeux n'ont plus de larmes pour crier pour vous, mes pauvres enfants. Adieu, adieu! . . . M.A.*'*

Henry William Paget, First Marquess of Anglesey (1768–1854), soldier and statesman, is remembered by most English schoolboys for the stories of his bravery at the Battle of Waterloo.

'By Gad, sir,' he is reputed to have said to Wellington as a French cannon ball flashed by, 'I believe I've lost my leg.'

'By Gad,' replied the Duke, looking down, 'I do believe you have.'

* '16 October, at 4.30 in the morning. My God! Have pity on me! There are no tears left in my eyes to cry for you, my poor children. Farewell, farewell! . . . M.A.'

Whether that cool exchange ever took place is doubtful, but Paget was certainly created a Marquess for his bravery during the battle. And there was obviously more to 'One Leg', as he was affectionately known, than his gallantry as a cavalry general, because he went on to become Lord Lieutenant of Ireland.

One of the possessions he bequeathed his descendants was an interesting library of books. The Pagets had been landed gentry for generations but had managed to inherit three titles in quick succession—as well as the houses that went with them. Part of the library was sold in the early 1900s. Recently, however, as part of the transaction which presented the family home to the National Trust, over a thousand books, typical of the eighteenth- and early nineteenth-century family reading, were purchased by the Howes Bookshop. Among them was the family Bible, with the signature of old 'One Leg' and his descendants in chronological order beneath. The Bible, well used but in good condition, is a huge tome published by John Baskerville (Cambridge 1763) and bound by John Baumgarten (d.1782), the Viennese who became the country's outstanding binder in the 'Chippendale' style, tooled in chinoiserie. The asking price of £1,500 is related mainly (surprising, some might think) to that Bible and its binding, and not to its association with the fascinating Marquess.

Sometimes one can judge the value of a book very easily, simply by using one's eyes to assess its aesthetic appeal—although in matters of beauty one is admittedly dependent to a certain extent on the dictates of fashion. There is no room in this study of the antiquarian-book world to deal properly with the vast subject of values and price fluctuations; in any case a dozen or so informative books have been devoted to the subject under the broad heading of 'collecting'. However, it would be useful to lightly sketch in the parameters so that we can relate them to other issues.

As I mentioned earlier, it is customary to equate prices with the record books, which means that generally it is easier to learn about books and manuscripts that break records than those which disappoint, or fail to reach the reserve price. Similarly, we become preoccupied by books and early authors appreciating in value, and drift away from those which fall by the wayside. Leaving aside works of great beauty, the older the book, the more we can rely on precedent; the newer (for example, modern first editions), the more we need judgement, and even then experts can be wrong. So we come back to the first law, which is buying what is likely to give you pleasure. Do not be concerned too much with so-called market prices; the market can be unpredictable, and that is something the dealers can worry about. A book that may be worth a small fortune today could be practically worthless tomorrow.

Ironically, some of the best buys originate from periods of relative disinterest. Take the Restoration, a tough time for publishing (compared with the theatre), with little incentive all round. Typically, John Milton (1608–74) an established and respected writer (his earliest poem *On the Death of a Fair Infant* was published in 1626), was paid a grand total of £15 for *Paradise Lost* (1667), and there was little evidence from immediate sales to indicate that he had been exploited. Today a first edition in decent condition would sell for little under £10,000. The experience of John Bunyan (1628–88) was very different. Whatever his financial reward (and that would not have worried him unduly), *Pilgrims' Progress* (1678, second part 1684) sold 100,000 copies within ten years, an incredible number for the seventeenth century, and went on to become one of the best sellers of all time. Strangely enough, despite the difference in the subjects they tackled, Bunyan was the Harold Robbins of his day, bringing the printed word to a great mass of people who might otherwise have read nothing apart from the Bible. Indeed, it was not until the early nineteenth century that the literary establishment led by Southey and Macauley belatedly accorded Bunyan the recognition he merited. Today a first edition of *Pilgrims' Progress* would probably be worth about £10,000 (£4,400 was paid in 1947). Bunyan's other books are relatively better value, partly because a fair proportion of his early published material has been destroyed, much of it during World War II.

Many authors are household names, but the famous can mean little in bookdealing, especially if their 'image' or style of writing is out of fashion, like John Galsworthy, George Bernard Shaw, and even Robert Burns (which seems incredible in view of his international reputation). The exception in his case is *Poems*,

Chiefly in the Scottish Dialect (1786), but only because the original binding was paper so that there are few copies left in complete order. If you have one in your attic, it could be worth several thousand pounds.

However, nothing can ever be taken for granted. In 1976 a set of letters exchanged by William Wordsworth and his wife Mary appeared on the market, to be hailed as a major literary find, since the passion displayed changed the portrait history had painted of a passive relationship in which the poet's sister Dorothy played a more romantic rôle than Mary. The letters came up for auction in London and, although the Dove Cottage Trust, which runs the Wordsworth museum at Grasmere in the Lake District, was unable to bid for lack of funds, it was estimated that the letters would fetch £100,000. But, on the day, bidding was so apathetic that the successful dealer, Seven Gables Bookshop of New York, representing an American university, had to go only to £35,000, barely above the reserve price. They were 'only' letters, true, but their literary significance is such that in other circumstances the sale price might have been doubled. At around the same time some autographed poems of William Morris failed to find a buyer.

Something which always has a ready market, is sex, or in literary terms 'erotica'. I referred earlier to the blind beggar who managed to 'see' the drawings he purchased—and even the printed word— but surely the most interesting handicap ever encountered must be that contained in the following extract from a New York bookseller's catalogue: 'First ed., published in Bombay: *Oriental Sex Practice* (spine damaged, appendix torn).'

John Sperr of Fisher and Sperr, Highgate, recalls one buying expedition where, among books stored in a garden shed, was a huge antiquarian volume with an integral lock. The spinster who owned the collection had no idea what the book was, or who had bequeathed it. When a suitable key was eventually found, they discovered a superb series of engraved erotica. With lock intact, the book is now in the possession of an Australian library.

The scarcity factor also makes a significant contribution to the inflated prices attained by such antiquarian material. Apart from limited print runs, when many respected collectors died certain items were removed and destroyed by well-meaning executors. A first edition of John Cleland's *Fanny Hill* (1748) is a good example.

Ironically, people sometimes go to incredible lengths to hide even ordinary books when under pressure. One bookseller remembers a scholarly customer who had a special deep pocket sewn into his overcoat so that he could conceal from his wife the books he needed, and which she regarded as an unnecessary extravagance. Regrettably, when the poor man died, his wife inherited a library of books worth a considerable sum. I do not know whether you would call that man an eccentric or merely henpecked.

But then what is eccentric? Have you heard the modern horror story of one Professor Jefferson, descendant of the American President, who had so many books in the house that he had to move out into the barn? The ill-fated gentleman continued collecting and collecting, until the ceiling collapsed and killed him. On the face of it, that sounds a little extraordinary, but surely we cannot all be experts on ceiling load-to-stress ratios! In fact, books 'taking over' in Triffid style is a common experience, even among booksellers who are supposed to be trained to cope with such hazards.

As a postal bookseller, I have had a number of strange customers, including several who judged the value of books by their size and weight alone: a twenty-fifth impression, cheap omnibus edition of short stories is considered good value at £5 if it has 600 pages or more, while a sixteenth-century leather-bound first edition is grossly overpriced at that figure if it has only fifty pages. Another client who collected the works of Mark Twain asked for his *A Tramp Abroad*, but on learning the publication date was 1880 declined our offer because 'it must be out of date by now'. A well known bookseller once sold the illustrations of William Blake (1757–1827) to Dante's *Inferno*, completed between 1314–19, because the customer was excited by the thought that Blake and Dante were contemporaries.

Whether the customer is eccentric or just ignorant, if he claims to know what he is talking about, the bookseller is surely free to exploit that man's so-called knowledge and obstinacy. Indeed, many people do not appreciate being corrected. Orioli mentions a client who would pay anything for incunabula with contemporary annotations in the margin, provided it was accompanied by a drawing of a hand with finger pointing at the text. This sort of margin note is not that unusual, but the collector was convinced that any books so marked must have come from the library of Francis Bacon—even when the text and the annotation were in different handwriting, or even in different languages.

J. N. Bartfield once received an order for a set of Gould, worth at that time about $10,000, scrawled on a sheet torn from a school notebook. Bartfield checked on the sender and discovered that he was genuine, and in fact had enough to cover the bill—more than enough, considering he actually owned a bank. The books were sent, and eventually a 'cheque' came back, written on a piece of brown paper cut from a bag. It was, of course, honoured.

Sometimes it is the behaviour of the trade which borders on eccentricity, particularly when it comes to recognising a desirable property. In the same way that many a best-selling novel has been turned down before one publisher, more 'perceptive' than the rest, took it up, so many opportunities to buy unusual material are passed up by booksellers and librarians. Charles P. Everitt, an American bookseller of some sixty years' experience (d.1950), had a bias against librarians—lack of 'imagination' being just one of their many alleged shortcomings. He gave a couple of examples of so-called shortsightedness in his *The Adventures of a Treasure Hunter* (1951). One reference is to a juvenile abbreviated edition of *Robinson Crusoe*—a book which has always fascinated me, partly because Daniel Defoe was sixty when it was published in 1719, and partly because of the awe-inspiring original title: *The Life and Strange Surprising Adventures of Robinson Crusoe, of York, Mariner, who eight-and-twenty years all alone in an uninhabited Island on the coast of America, near the Mouth of the Great River Oroonoque, having been cast on shore by Shipwreck, wherein all the men perished but himself; with an Account how he was at last strangely delivered by Pirates. Written by Himself.* *Robinson Crusoe* is probably the only one of Defoe's books worth 'big' money these days, except possibly *The Life of Captain Singleton* (1790), and it is this preoccupation with first-edition values that upset Everitt, who had offered to the New York Public library the rare children's edition, printed in New York in 1774, for $60. His initial contact at the library was excited by the find, and the amount required was approved by department heads. But the library director somehow became involved in the transaction and vetoed it on the grounds that public money could not be spared for a little children's book when they had other editions, including a first English edition. The assistant first approached was, however, given permission to buy the copy himself, and later sold it to a collector for $600, despite the fact that half the frontispiece was torn away.

Everitt also grumbled about his inability to sell the original manuscript for Bligh's *Mutiny on the Bounty*, which he had picked up for $50. The various institutions he approached with enthusiasm displayed little interest—the British Museum saying they had 'no money' (which is frequently true)—so that eventually he considered himself lucky to have got $500 from another bookseller. Much later, and too late, an Australian library popped up with an offer of £5,000.

An interesting sequel to the anecdote is that the original manuscripts of Bligh's record when his small party was set adrift —the voyage in the Bounty's launch—were bought in 1976 by John Maggs for the National Library of Sydney for £55,000. In auction parlance this fascinating pocket book of Bligh's was offered for sale by 'a gentleman', in fact a family descendant—his great grandfather having married Mary Jane Bligh, granddaughter of the infamous captain. In view of the significance of these papers—much of the information contained contradicts material already in possession of the Mitchell Library in Sydney, and the Manuscript Log and Journal in the possession of the Admiralty in London—part of the Christie's catalogue entry makes interesting reading:

BLIGH (LIEUTENANT WILLIAM): UNPUBLISHED AUTOGRAPH MS 'ROUGH ACCOUNT—LIEUTENANT WM. BLIGH'S VOYAGE IN THE BOUNTY'S LAUNCH FROM THE SHIP TO TOFUA & FROM THENCE TO TIMOR—', 28 April to 14 June 1789, THE ORIGINAL POCKET-BOOK FROM WHICH BLIGH WROTE ALL HIS SUBSEQUENT NARRA-

TIVES, OR, IN HIS OWN WORDS, 'This account was kept in my bosom as a common memorandum of our time & transposed into my fair Journal every day when the weather would admit with every material circumstance which passed.—Wm Bligh', written in the form of a Log and Journal in a notebook, which, as Bligh explains, belonged to Mr Hayward, who was with him in the launch, *the whole 107 pp., approx. 160mm × 100mm (water-staining, some edges frayed)*, including 1½ pages in Hayward's hand, probably Bligh's standing orders for signalling boats preceding the Bounty into anchorage, *with eight signal flags coloured red and blue, and crosshatched in Bligh's hand, 'This was part of our Signal Book wch. sat in Mr Hayward's pocket & served me to make my occurrences in—', a 3 pp. Prayer (with, immediately before it, a leaf excised), and 22½ pp* of Navigational Recordings and Calculations, EIGHT ROUGH SKETCH CHARTS OF ISLANDS, *one in pencil*, and showing the boat's track through the Barrier Reef and along the coast of Australia to the Torres Strait, *also* ONE AUTOGRAPH CHART HEADED 'EYE SKETCH OF PART OF NEW HOLLAND IN THE BOUNTY'S LAUNCH BY LIEUT. WM. BLIGH', *approx. 265mm × 183mm., bound in, and* THE AUTOGRAPH DRAFT LIST OF THE BOUNTY MUTINEERS, *3 folio leaves loosely inserted (water stained, neatly repaired, with loss of two words of text), later tree calf (rebacked), the first and last leaves of the text being probably the original wrappers of the Signal Book.*

After reproduction of the text and charts, with a note saying that the charts drawn in the manuscript appear to be unpublished, the list of mutineers is described thus:

... written on three loose folio sheets of regulation Admiralty issue paper, possibly torn out of Bligh's Journal, appears to be the Original Autograph Draft for the subsequent 'Description List of the Pirates remaining on board His Majesty's Armed Vessel Bounty on the 28 April 1789' ... The format, and in some places, the order of names and also the text, differ from the Admiralty MS. The untidy hand in which it is written, the deletions, insertions and ink-blots which appear on the pages all would seem to indicate that this was the first draft drawn up by Bligh, either at Coupang, or even while still in the Bounty's Launch. The manner in which Bligh exonerates Coleman, Byrne, McIntosh and Norman from culpability in the mutiny differs from the Admiralty version in which Coleman's declaration of innocence is embodied in the text where Bligh ends: 'These last McIntosh and Norman declared as Coleman had done—Michl. Byrne—I was told had no knowledge of what was doing—Wm Bligh'. While on the verso of the third sheet of the present MS, Bligh notes 'These—Joseph Coleman, Michl. Byrne—Thos. McIntosh and Chas. Norman are deserving of mercy being detained against their inclinations—Wm. Bligh'.

The existence of this important manuscript, the original source of all subsequent accounts of Bligh's passage to Timor, appears until recently to have been unknown outside Bligh's family. It is not mentioned in Bligh's own narrative nor in any of the authoritative works on Bligh. The only reference to such a pocket book is in James Morrison's *Journal* (ed. O. Rutter, 1935) where he describes the articles handed down to Bligh in the launch on the day of the mutiny: 'After Mr Bligh was in the boat he begged for his Commission and Sextant, the Commission was instantly given him with his Pocket Book and Private Journal by Mr Christian's orders . . .' Bligh himself, however, specifically states that 'it happened that a Mr Hayward had this Book with some signals sat [sic] down in it wch. appears in two Pages & I appropriated the blank leaves to this use'.

While the pocket book account is the same in substance as the published Admiralty manuscript (*The Log of the Bounty*, ed. O. Rutter, two volumes, 1936–7), there are textual differences arising from Bligh's subsequent 'writing up' of his experiences. Indeed the present manuscript emerges as a more poignant and in some ways more dramatic account of the epic voyage; it is a seaman's record of the difficulties and dangers of the passage, its bald statement of the facts being an expression of Bligh's struggles with the elements and of his skill as a navigator. Certain passages in the manuscript recording doubts and uncertainties do not appear in subsequent accounts; there are increasingly anxious notes, 'we now anxiously pray to make the land . . . no sight of land . . .', while earlier he records a prayer, 'O Lord our Heavenly Father Almighty . . . Receive us in this Night into thy Almighty protection . . . relieve us from our extreme distress, such as Men never felt . . .' Although the manuscript makes little mention of Bligh's difficulties with his men, in one unrecorded passage he breaks out in a cry of exasperation: 'Kind providence protects us wonderfully but it is a most unhappy situation to be in a Boat among such discontented People who don't know what to be at or what is best for them . . .' 'With its closely written pages of navigational recordings and reckoning, rough sketch charts and notes, the Bligh pocketbook provides the most complete navigational account yet known of the 3,500 mile voyage of the Bounty's launch from Tofua to Timor.'

That entry represents £55,000 and, although a direct comparison is not really valid, it does seem incredible that not so many years before, the authorities could have regarded the equivalent of £150 prohibitive.

Quite obviously any manuscript of historical significance is probably worth its weight in gold, so if you happen to stumble on an authenticated copy of Boadicia's battle orders please contact me without delay for personal advice! However, since it is far easier to win the pools or a national lottery, most booksellers prefer to set their sights a little lower, in the main on printed works more readily accessible. Some even endeavour to increase their chances by publishing material they have good reason to suppose will jump in value. When Quaritch dabbled in publishing —treating it as a straightforward business transaction—he plumped for William Morris, a combination that could not fail. Orioli, as much dabbler, full-time, at bookselling as dabbler, part-time, in publishing, first befriended the authors with whom he went into partnership, men of the stature of Norman Douglas, D. H. Lawrence, Somerset Maugham and Richard Aldington. Their books were published from Florence.

Orioli's taste was impeccable and, of those three, only Maugham fell by the wayside as a 'collector's author'. A homosexual, Orioli's relationship with the talented Douglas (whom he describes vividly in *Moving Along*) was most probably intimate, and it enabled him to begin his publishing venture in 1930 with *Nerinda*. Most of Douglas' better works had been written before this period (*South Wind*, 1917, is considered by many to be a masterpiece), but the first edition of 475 copies quickly sold out. It is, of course, this type of small print-run that subsequently boosts the price of first editions when an author becomes collectable.

Orioli's relationship with Lawrence, whom he had originally met in England, is more difficult to comprehend. He was a regular visitor at the Villa Mirenda when Lawrence was working on *Lady Chatterley's Lover*, and indeed drew ten per cent of his royalties for acting as an on-the-spot editor-cum-publisher. However, the first Lawrence book with which he was entrusted was a translation of Lasca's *Story of Dr Manente*, which launched his Lungarno series, and was a flop—largely because of the author's ego, which prompted him to demand that 2,400 copies be printed. *The Virgin and the Gipsy*, however, was oversubscribed, possibly because it came out soon after his death, and people imagined it would be as erotic as *Lady Chatterley's Lover*.

But picking an author whose books will appreciate dramatically in value is just as difficult as predicting success in any of the arts. In his lifetime Shaw was as respected as he was popular; when he died, interest in his books plummetted. Generally, the more prolific a writer, the less he would seem to be accepted by the literary establishment (J. B. Priestley is a good example) which seems to dictate collecting trends. Lawrence, along with Evelyn Waugh and Graham Greene are among the few exceptions, although they did not exactly churn out their work.

It must be conceded, however, that, in our rather smug, esoteric dissertations on 'literary stature' and 'market values', most of us begin to relate books to merchandise, dismissing the *raison d'être* of the book and the author's stake in the affair. I do not suppose that Harold Robbins cares very much if his books are not in demand in the twenty-first century, so long as they stay at the top of the bestseller list in his lifetime. Equally, it is small consolation to the thousands of writers who could not survive if they had to manage on their royalties to know that one day in the distant future their talents might be appreciated. The idea that hardship improves the mind—as in the traditional picture of the author starving in his garret—is too ridiculous to merit discussion.

William Hutton (1723–1815), the English bookseller who became better known as writer, had a childhood so sordid it makes *Oliver Twist* seem as light-hearted as a French farce. His start in bookselling was almost as tough, until he had his first break: he moved to Nottingham where a kindly clergyman took pity on him, and, realising he could not afford to amass a decent stock, sold him two hundredweight of books at his own price, with payment to be postponed. The 'contract' actually read 'I promise to pay Ambrose Rudsall £1 7s od [£1.35] when I am able'. The story had, incidentally, a happy ending, but it serves to illustrate that the bookworld is not usually the bed of roses it might seem.

Of course, we cannot always judge hardship by superficial appearances. Some people, especially obsessive collectors, might seem impoverished simply because they spend all their money on books. Sidney Smith, a much respected London bookseller, was once asked to 'clear' the flat of a customer friend who had recently died. The deceased's tiny accommodation was exceptionally cramped by normal standards, but inside Smith found over 35,000 books, mainly antiquarian—considerably in excess of the stock carried by most bookshops—leaving just enough room for the occupant to eat and move between living room and bedroom. The setting might have been lifted straight from the pages of Arnold Bennett's *Riceyman Steps*, except that in the basement were even more books and some 100,000 loose prints, as well as photograph albums, mostly ruined by damp. I think it particularly poignant when a collector dies before getting a chance to at least sort out the books on which he has lavished much love over the years, and perhaps donate or even sell them to someone appreciative.

The subject of death brings me finally to life *after* death; in other words, the spirit world. One cannot leave book 'tales' without a brief mention of a couple of haunted premises in the UK. One ghost is reported to inhabit the premises of William Smith, booksellers since 1832 at Reading in Berkshire. Part of the building dates back to the seventeenth century, when it was used as a meeting house for Quakers, one member of the congregation being William Penn. The ghost—like most of his kind, seldom around when wanted—has been seen by staff, dressed in the Quaker 'uniform' of sombre black, with a steeple crowned hat and large white collar.

The other, spotted in an underground passage below Sanders of Oxford—originally a sixteenth-century pilgrim's hostel—could be even older, since witnesses have only been able to describe a 'monkish apparition'. Unfortunately this gentleman is even more elusive, so it is hardly worth making a special visit, unless by some spiritual pre-arrangement.

5 The Common Enemy: The Book Thief

The Shoe Lane end of Holborn Viaduct in London is not a busy shopping thoroughfare at the best of times. In the evening and at weekends it is positively deserted, vulnerably so, as it transpired, for Thomas Thorp, which has one of the country's most impressive stocks of what it describes as 'rare and interesting' books. Thorp, which has an equally well known 'sister' shop in Guildford, Surrey, had moved a few years before from prestigious West End premises where it had been based for thirty years of almost a century in the business. The shop has a friendly atmosphere; its staff comes from the traditional school yet has none of the usual pomp and ceremony; and, most important, it offers real scope for the serious browser in a wide range of subjects—a facility that attracts customers from all over the world. One weekend in September 1977 the shop attracted collectors of a more sinister variety: break-in specialists who left with 26,000 volumes, worth many thousands of pounds—the most breathtaking, and unquestionably the bulkiest, book theft of all time.

The thieves broke in through a skylight and dropped or climbed down a rope into the shop before systematically emptying the locked bookcases full of the better books, levering open those with steel shutters before moving on to the ordinary shelves. Their haul included everything from rare fifteenth- and sixteenth-century material to 'popular' antiquarian books of a general nature, such as the first editions of the famous nineteenth-century novelists. Yet it would seem that the thieves had no concept of individual values because, apart from basic assumptions (for example, that more valuable books would be kept in locked bookcases), they appear to have been concerned with the systematic clearance of the shop rather than with individual titles. Parts of valuable sets were left behind.

The shop has a large front window on the main road, and the men must have worked in full view of the infrequent passers-by, although presumably there would have been nothing to distinguish them from shop assistants working overtime. The books must have been taken through a back door into a yard at a lower level to a waiting lorry or van.

Regrettably the shop, while insured for the customary fire and flood, did not have cover for theft of this magnitude: few people in the trade had ever contemplated the possibility of theft on such a scale. A list of some of the more important titles was circulated to members of the Antiquarian Booksellers' Association, but all were unmarked and, apart from a handful of very rare items, many titles could confidently be offered to reputable bookshops who were not members. The police worked on the theory that the men were acting on instructions from an expert who would have the books shipped in bulk to the Continent for re-sale, rather than try to offload them in small numbers.

However, although many antiquarian books are lost by such (albeit smaller scale) burglaries, shop-lifting and thefts from libraries account for the greatest number of thefts, in terms of volume and value. The annual loss of antiquarian works is considerably more significant than people realise, and the problem is far more complex than that facing retail stores in the big shopping centres—partly because a stolen pair of pants has a smaller re-sale value than an interesting book, but more important, because it can always be replaced.

Admittedly, the better known an antiquarian book, the less opportunity there is to sell it legitimately, although even that is not a deterrent to the determined thief. The Gutenberg Bible at Harvard University was actually removed from the Houghton Library, and the thief would have got away from the premises if the rope by which he was climbing had not broken under the additional weight of the enormous Bible. The motive in that case was not sale but ransom, and this has become an increasing danger in recent years. Also there are undoubtedly collectors, every bit as dishonest as those we read about in fiction, who would give anything to possess something they might never show to another soul.

At the other end of the scale, since paperbacks are also a target of certain book thieves, we can only assume that the motive is not always to collect the rare! A bookseller in Charing Cross Road remembers a young woman who came in every day to browse among the paperbacks, usually settling for one and reading a couple of pages each day until she had finished the story. If it did not meet with her approval she would return it to the shelves; if she liked it, the paperback would simply disappear. Small wonder many booksellers are inclined towards cynicism.

Of course, in the West we take certain things for granted, and, although rapidly gaining respectability, principally for economic reasons, paperbacks might still be regarded as rather down-market. In other less fortunate countries they have the novelty of a treasure trove; at Moscow's first international book fair in September 1977 exhibitors lost more copies to pilferers than to the Soviet customs men, the greatest attraction apparently being Penguins.

Among the various categories of book thief there is the regular but still amateur crook who thinks there is little wrong in stealing from a big bookshop since 'everybody' does it, and 'they' make a huge profit in any case, so 'they' do not miss a few odd books. This type, kidding himself that what he does is more 'one-upmanship' than stealing, is often genuinely interested in books, and is, therefore, probably friendly with his local corner book-store which, through respect and admiration for the owner, he would never dream of robbing.

So the book thief ranges from the run-of-the-mill klepto-maniac through the bibliophile submitting to momentary temptation to the professional thief (be he a shoplifter or a burglar). Sudden temptation is something experienced by almost every bibliophile at one time in his life, myself included; varying degrees of self-control being the one quality that separates us from thieves. Even booksellers have succumbed. One well known West End dealer was asked to value an eighteenth-century volume of Swiss colour prints, fell in love with it on the spot, and later told the owner the book had been lost. He was charged, found guilty, heavily fined and, worse, his reputation in the trade was destroyed overnight. The man is not only a good bookseller but a warm-hearted, likeable person having to live down a momentary lapse in self-discipline.

As I suggested earlier, booksellers as a breed are an honest bunch, more sinned against than sinners. I am reminded of an occasion in the early 1970s when Peter Kay of Joseph's bought at auction the twenty-four-volume Nonesuch Press edition of Dickens, illustrated by contemporary artists of the calibre of Cruikshank and Phiz. The feature of the set (worth about a thousand pounds today) was that the last volume was phoney, used for housing a steel plate, wrapped in cotton wool, of one of the original illustrators, together with one 'pull', and a letter of authentication. The set was in less than perfect condition and the price therefore set at 'only' £550; but on examining it closely on the second day of the sale (a Friday) Kay discovered the plate was missing. Not really interested in an incomplete set, he nevertheless offered to pay a reduced sum and the offer was accepted. However, on Monday morning, on opening the shop, the plate was discovered having been slipped through the letter box by a conscience-stricken thief. Many people might have been tempted to remain silent and make a substantial profit, since there was no way for anyone to find out. But Joseph's immediately contacted the auctioneers and paid the full price.

'Dedicated' and experienced book thieves do not need to rely on obvious ploys like the briefcase and the raincoat over the arm. Books have been hidden in concealed pockets, smaller editions tucked into socks, and prints wrapped around the body under a jumper. At Hodgson's Saleroom (part of Sotheby's) the staff had been suspicious of one regular customer interested in the topography of the Cinque ports; this narrow interest proved his undoing since these were the books that usually went missing, although he was never 'caught in the act'. Eventually the staff set a trap, sending one of their number up into the gallery from which he was able to watch everything below through a skylight. The thief was spotted this time pushing a book down the front of his trousers. At his home, police also found between thirty and forty books stolen from another bookseller who, when questioned by police, admitted that he had actually caught the thief on an earlier occasion, and let him go when the man returned some hundred other volumes stolen in the past!

Other shops can often include an additional percentage in their retail prices to offset losses through shoplifting, but this is not practical in the book trade; the tendency is either to restrict the customers' freedom to browse or to lock away expensive books (which presumably leaves the thief free to pilfer general stock in the one to fifty pounds range). But even a safe or strong room is not foolproof. One major West End firm has a strong room to which only twenty to thirty of their most valued customers were ever admitted; it is now out-of-bounds to everyone, unless accompanied by a member of staff, following the theft of an important book. Since the theft was not discovered immediately the staff were unable to pinpoint the date or the visitors over the relevant period, and therefore all special customers came under suspicion.

Some of those customers may have been rich or distinguished men. Indeed, it is the apparent respectability of so many book thieves that confuses the trade. Booksellers are only human and tend to be suspicious of scruffy-looking individuals; one dealer of my acquaintance was very worried on one occasion when a particularly long haired and wild-bearded young man piled up a huge assortment of items, only to discover that not only was he titled but also he was certainly not short of a pound or two. The same bookseller inevitably hesitates to ask a distinguished academician to turn out his pockets simply because he has been buried in a hidden corner of the shop for a couple of hours.

The problem is that apart from an alarm system, such as that which the Antiquarian Booksellers' Association has for alerting booksellers (although this only applies to members, a respected but relatively small section of the trade) or that operated by the libraries, there is very little of practical value the trade can do to stop large-scale theft. A working party was set up in 1972 by the Antiquarian Booksellers' Association and the Rare Books Group of the Library Association; certain sensible recommendations were made but thefts continue to increase. This knowledgeable and down-to-earth committee was originally chaired by Howard Nixon, then Deputy Keeper of Printed Books at the British Museum and now librarian to the Westminster Abbey library. It comprised two librarians, an archivist and three booksellers, one of whom had books stolen while he was sitting on the committee! Critics might have preferred to see one or two full-time professional crimebusters seconded; the committee did listen to experts in the different aspects of security. To be fair, we are dealing with a problem that, in terms of security, is virtually impossible to solve. To secure a property one locks it away, but books are placed in shops for sale, and in libraries for reference, which in both cases means accessibility.

The working party began by making the reasonable assumption that, since the value of rare books continues to grow fairly sharply, then the incidence of crime was likely to continue at least at the same rate and probably faster. They noted that, since the majority of stolen items were then offered for sale, it was the bookseller on whom the financial loss fell when those items were recovered.

Maggs Brothers of Berkeley Square, London, perhaps the most prestigious antiquarian bookseller still controlled by one family, have been on the receiving end of a number of pieces of skullduggery and one was especially bizarre. Managing director John Maggs, a fourth-generation bookseller, estimates that in a few years, the company had in good faith bought over twenty thousand pounds worth of books, stolen from such places as the British Museum, the Literary and Philosophical Society of Newcastle-upon-Tyne, the Northumberland Record Office, the Wellcome Institute, the Patent Office, and the Middle Temple library. All were in turn sold, which meant that the money subsequently had to be repaid. In his office I was shown a fairly ordinary academic book bought at an auction, but which he had later suspected had been stolen from a school library. 'I've checked with the school, but they deny it,' he said, 'and the auction house claims it doesn't have time to check these things in advance.'

In 1970 Maggs bought several items from an American PhD who was studying at Newcastle. Maggs was just one of several

reputable bookshops taken in by this prepossessing young man
who claimed the books were from a collection gathered together
by his grandfather. His explanation much later was that he was
less interested in financial profit than in trying to associate his
family name with scholarship by establishing the credibility of his
family tree. The fact that he netted £9,000 on the books seems
conveniently to have escaped his attention. His taste, incidentally,
was impeccable, as the following 'stock' list indicates:

> From the Library of the School of Fine Art, two wood blocks
> by Thomas Bewick (*The Chillingham Bull*, and, *Waiting for
> Death*), and valuable eighteenth-century chapbooks.
> From the University Library, Bullein, *Bulwarke of Defence*,
> London 1562; Fuchs, *De Historia Stirpium*, Basileae 1542; de
> L'Orme, *Premier tome de l'architecture*, Paris 1567; Turner,
> *Herbal*, Collen 1568; Adam, *R & J Works*, London 1778–86,
> two volumes folio.
> From the Library of the Literary and Philosophical Society,
> Gould, *Birds of Australia*, 1848–59, 8 volumes folio; Gould,
> *A century of birds from Himalaya Mountains*, 1831–32, one
> volume folio.

The young man turned up at Maggs with one of the Goulds and
a Sarum Missal of 1420. The staff at any decent antiquarian bookshop are not especially gullible, and need more than a plausible
story before they hand over money, but not only had he devised a
foolproof background, he had had a library bookplate made
around his grandfather's initials, 'AB', circled with laurel leaves
and heavily embossed, large enough to cover the true ownership
stamp. Maggs sold the Missal to an Amsterdam dealer for £1,000
and, when the student was arrested, they recalled it and refunded
the dealer's money.

The irony of this particular anecdote is that the true ownership
of the Missal has never been established. It was assumed that
the convicted man had stolen it, but he refused to talk beyond
generalities and, despite considerable publicity within the bookworld, no one has ever claimed it. There must come a time when
Maggs will feel that ownership has reverted to them, and that

they are at liberty to re-sell the Missal, but after ten years they have still not taken that decision. One sad thought is that a bookseller, who unwittingly pays several thousand pounds and cannot recoup his money through the usual sales channels, has no recourse other than to sue the thief in a civil court when he leaves prison—and that, obviously, would not get him very far.

The working party therefore had two principal objectives, to make theft more difficult and to make the sale of stolen books more difficult, thus 'discouraging' the thief. They restricted their attention to valuable books and manuscripts, defined as those having a saleable value of over fifty pounds. Books below this price level are stolen in large numbers, but understandably the working party had to draw the line somewhere. A useful tip I picked up when researching my *Book Browser's Guide* was from a dealer who priced all his 'rubbish' at ten pounds or more in the hope that less perceptive book thieves would take them off his hands! Detailed information and evidence examined by the working party, including the areas of mechanical aids (locks, keys and alarms), and the marking of books and documents (the various types of stamp and perforation), were supplied by such experts as J. Manning, Security Advisor to the National Museums and Art Galleries, A. D. Baynes-Cope of the British Museum Research Laboratory, and Nigel Seeley of the Metropolitan Police Laboratory.

For obvious reasons I am not prepared to disclose the technical advice provided, although I am sure there is little the professional crook is not aware of, but the working party came to the following conclusions:

all valuable books and documents should be marked in some way;
they should be seen to be marked;
the marking should be as difficult as possible to remove;
it is desirable to have some special, less obvious means of identification, such as the use of invisible ink, or a small inconspicuous stamp or perforation on a specified page in the middle of the book, which may not be noticed by a thief when removing more obvious marks;

all valuable plates, maps or insertions in a book should also
be marked;
the marks *must* be cancelled, not obliterated if the book is
disposed of; and
it is the responsibility of a bookseller, or other purchaser, to
check with the library concerned, any book bearing an un-
cancelled mark of ownership.

Howard Nixon recalls that, up until the time of the working
party, a number of important books at the British Museum had
not been stamped, and the committee heard evidence that one of
the three known copies of the first edition of the *Marseillaise* had
been stolen from the Museum by an 'academically inclined' thief
(professional enough to have planned it in Wormwood Scrubs
prison) who was a regular visitor to the British Museum reading
room, and as such familiar with its routine. It was stolen on a
Saturday, but recovered in the left-luggage office of Baker Street
station on the following Monday because the thief was not aware
of one additional check which took place.

Many booksellers blame librarians for creating the climate in which
it is relatively easy to steal. Sometimes, they admit, the fault is not
that of the individual: a librarian may not have been at his job for
long and therefore be not fully aware of the extent of his stock, or
a large collection may have been added to the library and not yet
catalogued. But, more often, libraries and college authorities are
accused of endeavouring to maintain a dignified silence, either to
protect the body from unwelcome publicity or because they wish
to 'cover up' if the theft is proved to have been an inside job—out
of shame, of course, not dishonesty.

The flaws in the organisation of libraries are illustrated by the
anecdotes given earlier about the Scottish University bidding for
an extremely rare volume of poems, when they already had the
only other copy in their possession, and the American library
unable to assist Canon Fitch's search for the missing parochial
library books because so many had not yet been catalogued. (The
Houghton Library of Harvard, and the University Library at
Austin, Texas—which, appropriately enough in this context,

houses the world's largest collection of detective fiction—are typical of excellent university libraries which have bought so extensively over the years that cataloguing must always be an uphill struggle. Bill Jackson of Harvard is regarded by many authorities as an outstanding librarian largely because of the time he spent buying, in the belief that the supply would eventually dry up. Equally, it has been said that many smaller United States universities have overspent and may, sooner or later, as overheads continue to rise, have to offload some of their books—but that is another issue.)

University libraries offering access to original research material are an obvious target and, while it would be wrong to compile a thief's league table, the major establishments of learning obviously come out near the top. Harvard had a narrow escape with the Gutenberg Bible. Yale have had their share of thefts but maintain a veil of secrecy. Still, they were unable to avoid publicity when in 1973 a large number of rare books and illuminated manuscripts were stolen, although later recovered. What made the story front-page news was the fact that the thieves were two former Greek Orthodox priests, and their motive was to help finance the release of some colleagues behind the Iron Curtain! Not so far away, at Dartmouth College in New Hampshire, some old maps valued at around $75,000 were stolen in 1974 by an antique dealer who left them in a 'bus terminal locker from which they were recovered. Lockers seem to be a popular hiding place in the United States because a robbery of similar proportions, in this case prints and art books, ended with an anonymous telephone call to the police identifying a locker in Grand Central station, although this time the thief was not apprehended.

Oxford and Cambridge, while losing no masterpieces, have suffered a spate of losses, particularly in the area of valuable maps and colour plates—with or without the books that housed them. The thief who had his eye on Boydell's *History of the River Thames* at Queen's College, Oxford, picked the wrong time to swoop because Volume One was out at the time (for genuine research) and he had to make do with Volume Two. For consolation he took an Ackerman's *Cambridge*.

The astuteness of an assistant at Blackwell's antiquarian

department in Oxford prevented another significantly large theft. Among thirty volumes brought into the shop for sale was a copy of Locke's *Human Understanding*, which the assistant recognised to be of a particular issue of which there were only two or three surviving copies. Suspicious that an 'ordinary' collector should have such an unusual edition, the assistant accepted the books on approval and asked that the vendor come back for the money. The volume was rushed round to a local expert on shelf-marks, who identified not only the book but the college from which it had been stolen. (The college, incidentally, did not know the book had gone.)

Cambridge was once the scene of a rather more 'luck rather than judgement' style of detective work. Galloway and Porter, the old-established booksellers we have already mentioned, reported the loss of ten bound volumes of the fourteen-volume *Curtis Botanical Magazine* (valuable because of the plates) and a first edition of W. B. Yeats. Nothing was heard of the books for two years, until a news snippet in the *Cambridge News* referred to a mysterious parcel found in a bicycle shed beside one of the college libraries. The parcel was addressed to an Irish university but not stamped—the thief must have either lost his nerve, run out of money for stamps, or simply forgotten where he had left the parcel!

Maggs were once offered an illuminated manuscript which had the number of one of their own catalogues written in pencil inside the front cover. There was no reason why a legitimate purchaser should necessarily have erased the mark, but in this instance it proved a thief's mistake. The shop decided to check by looking up that old catalogue, and discovered the book had been sold to Liverpool Cathedral Library. They contacted the library to ascertain whether or not it had recently sold the book; once again, here was a library that did not even know the book had disappeared.

It must be conceded that even the most security conscious librarian can do little if not only the book but the index card is stolen or if someone merely takes the plates from a book rarely consulted. The Antiquarian Booksellers' Association working party's suggestion that every plate be marked in a library copy provides a deterrent, but it is too unsightly for the bookseller who is concerned with selling copies in as attractive a condition as possible. However, marking may well be the best solution because, if it is almost impossible to prevent the determined professional thief getting what he wants—even the most sophisticated alarm system can be beaten—at least it makes it slightly easier to stop him reaping the rewards. One compromise marker-cum-alarm tried, but largely discarded, is to insert a magnetised metal strip in the spine of a book; this, if it has not been demagnetised, activates an alarm when taken past a control point. But the professional will look for it and deactivate it himself, or, as a couple of firms discovered, someone can forget to insert the strip in the first place.

There are, of course, occasions when no one cares anyway. Arms & Armour, the London mail-order specialists, once received a rare copy, one of only a dozen privately published by an American millionaire to commemorate his important collection of firearms. Only a few of these were distributed to selected people, so that when one turned up bearing the stamp of a United States library Lionel Leventhal, the managing director of Arms & Armour, was suspicious. On checking, he discovered that the book *had* been stolen, but that the librarian was undisturbed by the loss since he regarded the book as totally without interest or value. Arms & Armour subsequently catalogued the item at £500 and promptly received seven orders. (The pricing of a book, as I said earlier, is an interesting and controversial issue. In this case, there was nothing to go on, and £1,000 may well have been equally acceptable to certain collectors.)

However, missing books do not necessarily have to be stolen. The working party quotes from a letter from an Oxford bookseller, Albi Rosenthal, who had spotted an English fifteenth-century text manuscript at a Swiss antiquarian bookshop and thought it would be of interest to the Bodleian Library:

> I left it with Dr Hunt, Keeper of Western MSS, on approval.
> The MS was in a recent full morocco binding, and had an
> armorial engraved book-plate stuck inside the cover, which
> bore only a date: 1701. After several days, Dr Hunt appeared

at my office with the MS under his arm, and a catalogue of Queen's College Library, Cambridge, printed at the beginning of the century in which this MS was described. The coat of arms had been identified at Bodley as that of a Peer of the Realm who had bequeathed his books to Queen's College, early in the eighteenth century.

I immediately wrote to the librarian of the College, asking whether this MS had been sold since it was catalogued, or not. He rang me up on the following day, requesting the return of this MS which was last checked as being in the College in 1945. I assured him that, although I had no authority to hand over the MS (the book had not been purchased at this stage), I would do all I could to clear the matter up and see that it would, in due course, be returned to the College.

I was then able to retrace its recent history through a public auction at Parke-Bernet, and two other previous owners, both booksellers. One of them had purchased it several years before it came into my hands, at Sotheby's. They identified the 'perfectly respectable' Cambridge antique dealer who had sent in the MS for auction. What finally emerged was that a Fellow of the College, who had the right to take the MS into his rooms, had died whilst the book was on his shelves, and it was sold by mistake with the rest of his books to this antique dealer. There was no library stamp by which the provenance could have been identified.

Life can be even more complicated when, for example, in the case of a family heirloom it is impossible to decide on the ownership of a book. One grand-nephew's claim is no stronger than that of his brother, or perhaps his widow, especially when there have been several generations involved. And if the family goes back to the Middle Ages it may well have stolen ('appropriated') the book or manuscript by right of conquest in the first place. It is said that Catherine de Medici stole many of the books in her library of over 4,000 volumes. Ironically, on her death the books were in danger of being seized by her creditors, but her almoner took them to his own home and they were then placed in the royal library. Catherine's coat of arms and cypher were first removed—so if you should run across a couple of 'complete' copies, you will have struck lucky.

I have often referred to colour-plate books. In 1976, the great expert on these, Charles Traylen had a five-volume set of Gould's *Birds of Britain*, marked at £8,000, stolen from his Guildford shop, and, despite a reward of £500 for information alone, the set has never been recovered. It had been taken out of the strong-room to show to a customer and then placed in the window for a week. The vision so inspired one windowshopper that he came back at night, forced a window at the back and took the Gould (and nothing else). To rub salt into the wounds, Traylen discovered in the small print of his insurance policy that cover extended only as far as the doors of the strongroom. Subsequently police actually traced twenty-five Gould plates, offered for sale in Oxford, that had been cut from a book with a razor blade. Until he can match up the jagged edges with those of the book from which they were cut, Traylen has no means of knowing whether they are really his.

The problem is not simply to make books less accessible, because the determined thief is not put off by what others would regard as obstacles. Even in a small shop, with expensive books displayed in cabinets, customers would have to be kept under constant observation to lessen the risks. At the A. J. Cumming shop in Lewes, Sussex, during one busy day in 1977, the staff was diverted from a large display cabinet, normally in full view, just long enough for one customer to slip a hand inside and remove an item that attracted him. The stolen book, a calf-bound copy of Defoe's little known *The Secrets of the Invisible World Disclosed* (1729), with a number of attractive engraved plates, was the nearest to hand on opening the cabinet, which led the owner and police to assume that the thief had acted on the spur of the moment, since other more expensive volumes were more difficult to reach—they were also larger and heavier, which might have been another deterrent.

Valuable books have also been taken from private collections. Milton's cottage in Chalfont St Giles, Buckinghamshire, UK, now a museum and shrine to the writer, was broken into in 1977, and nineteen rare books stolen, including first editions of *Paradise*

Lost (1667) and *Paradise Regained* (1671). The cottage, used by Milton as a refuge from the plague, was entered at night by forcing the leaded windows to the study where the books were kept. The burglar or burglars obviously knew what to look for, and were exceptionally quiet (the curator and his wife were sleeping on the premises but heard nothing). The first editions were kept in a barred and locked cabinet within a larger locked cabinet, but this seems to have presented no major difficulty. The monetary value of the collection is small, little over £1,500, but to Milton enthusiasts the loss is incalculable.

At much the same time, police were investigating at a house in Berkshire the disappearance from one of the country's most impressive private collections of a limited edition of T. E. Lawrence's *Seven Pillars of Wisdom*, worth about £2,000. The copy, signed by Lawrence and published in 1920, had in addition to the colour plates, an extra colour plate of Brickley Pair, not indexed. Despite a substantial reward offered by the owner, detectives were not optimistic about ever finding the copy, suspecting it had fallen into the hands of an unscrupulous collector. Because of the size of the library, the book could have been taken over a three month period, which means it could have been the work of a burglar, a visitor, or even a member of the staff.

The audacity of thieves and tricksters, not only in stealing but in re-selling their haul, would be amusing if it were not so disturbing in a trade which cannot afford these losses. Someone walked into Bertram Rota's old premises in London's Savile Row a few years ago during the national miners' strike, which caused power cuts throughout the United Kingdom. Taking advantage of the candlelight he produced a beautiful copy of the Golden Cockerel (private) Press edition of the *Four Gospels*, bound in half-white pigskin and maize buckram sides. Because of this exceptionally light coloured binding, existing copies are usually fairly grubby, but a fine copy is worth about £850—which was the price demanded by the confidence trickster. In normal light, the fact that the book had recently been rebound would have been immediately apparent to experienced eyes, but in the flickering shadows of the candles the staff had to look long and hard before deciding it was a fake. Once they had decided, they got their own back by dragging out the examination to extraordinary lengths, insisting on hearing the opinion of even the office junior while the vendor sweated. (In fact, here there might have been an interesting point of law, because it is no crime to go to the original binder to have a book recovered in the same materials and style; it becomes dishonest only when one attempts to pass it off as the original binding.)

Thieves are not always motivated by bibliomania or financial profit. Arms & Armour, mentioned earlier, who took on the collection of the late Ken Trotman, recognised as perhaps the great authority in the field, lost much of that potential profit overnight through an assistant. On checking with their binders to ascertain why certain valuable books had not been returned, they found that they had not been sent in the first place. Further investigation revealed that an assistant had taken them home, ostensibly for cataloguing, and kept them. After questioning, the assistant, later found to be mentally unbalanced, admitted she had not only not catalogued them, she had *burned* them— rare items including some vellum bound sixteenth-century manuscripts.

Personally, I would place book thieves in two main categories: the specialist to whom the book is merely a vehicle for making money, and whose interest in the stolen property is purely professional; and the crooked bibliophile, or bibliomaniac, epitomised by that Don Vincente who stabbed his customers to death merely to get his books back.

In the case of the former, there is very little we can do. After all, as he would say: 'It's nothing personal. I'm only trying to earn a living!' To the latter we might, however, appeal for a greater measure of self-control. Perhaps morals do not come into it, but most book lovers share a sense of romanticism. And surely, to most of us, much of the joy of collecting is synonymous with the desire and pursuit of one's vision. Of course, we want to possess the things we desire, but half the fun disappears when that object is presented to us on a plate.

It may sound pretentious to say that the satisfaction of finding and producing a very scarce book for a customer, is one of the highlights of bookselling that makes it all worthwhile; but it's a fact. Indeed, there are those in bookshops who maintain that the reward of seeing the customer's delighted expression, is what bookselling is all about, and why they would never wish to lose that face-to-face contact. That is why the impersonal business of mail order bookselling is considered by the same people to be little different to any other ordinary office job.

But the point is that if a book is easy to come by, there is no need to get excited. Who has ever heard of even the most single-minded bibliophile jumping up and down with joy at getting a new publication hot off the presses? Far greater satisfaction comes from the suspense of waiting, coupled with the eventual realisation of one's dream. Even books that are virtually unobtainable will excite us so long as they are fractionally beyond reach. Simply presented to us, unexpectedly, and in false circumstances, they are merely something of an anti-climax.

Andrew Lang's *Ballade of the Unattainable* makes this point more eloquently:

> *The books I cannot hope to buy*
> *Their phantomes round me waltz and wheel,*
> *They pass before the dreaming eye*
> *Ere sleep the dreaming eye can seal.*
> *A kind of literary reel*
> *They dance; how fair the bindings shine!*
> *Prose cannot tell them what I feel—*
> *The Books that never can be mine!*

6 The Detective at Bay

In the days before book editors, when titles and chapter headings were allowed a half-page in their own right, I think I might have embellished that bare heading with a series of explanatory sub-titles. The subject of this chapter, literary forgeries, is far more complex than one initially imagines; probably more so with regard to books than in any other art form. If we begin, for example, with definitions, the opposite of 'copy' is 'original', yet original in this context does not necessarily mean genuine.

The dictionary defines 'genuine' as 'pure-bred; really coming from its reputed source', but how does that relate to authors who are themselves figments of the imagination? There have been several instances of literary forgers inventing writers and illustrators of a past age, which means there was no genuine source to start with. In the case of an invented writer, why should a masterpiece attributed to him suddenly lose value when declared a forgery? The answer is that we tend to judge in terms of so-called 'market values' which are not necessarily the same as the true ones.

Expert opinion has, in any case, proved to be highly vulnerable in the arts and, although it has become almost impossible to reproduce very old books and manuscripts because of scientific advances in the study of manual and mechanical printing techniques, papers and inks, the literary content is another matter. In common with most experts, even the knowledgeable bookseller can be hoodwinked—not because he is especially gullible, but because like any enthusiastic treasure hunter he subconsciously wants to believe in the authenticity of a valuable find.

Only a few years ago the American novelist Clifford Irving produced the 'memoirs' of the multimillionaire recluse, Howard Hughes; it was a brilliant hoax for which he subsequently served a term in prison. But, quite apart from the fact that Irving's part-fiction/part-fact biography was a fascinating piece of authorship, he actually forged letters purportedly written by Hughes and shown by the publishers to handwriting consultants who compared them with authentic material. On seeing the real thing Irving was so appalled by his ineptitude as a handwriting forger that he dashed home and recopied the fakes. Yet the experts had been totally convinced by his first effort, and were subsequently unaware of the overnight change in that evidence. Admittedly, there was big money at stake in that publishing operation, and this may have clouded judgements to some degree, but the memoirs would have been published and Irving's fraud probably never exposed (unless Hughes had uncharacteristically stepped into the limelight) had it not been for a quirk of fate unrelated to his work. Irving's huge royalty advances had been paid into a Swiss bank account in his wife's name. It was only when this information was surprisingly revealed (contrary to the tradition of Swiss banking) that his plans collapsed.

But what is authenticity without tangible proof? Name and reputation mean nothing, rightly, since so many villains have concealed their activities behind a façade of respectability. Can we trust the famous? Take Shakespeare, for example. I am not suggesting that England's greatest writer was a fraud, a mere hack who copied the style, and even words, of his literary peers (take your pick of them), but no one can deny that, at times, his vocabulary seems remarkably similar to Marlowe's. In fact, I side with Shakespeare and his supporters, but enough controversy has been generated over the years by dedicated non-believers to create some element of doubt. Even so, I have yet to encounter any bookseller who refuses to stock Shakespeare's plays on that account! Others have tried, unsuccessfully, to write plays in William's name. Mind you, even if it could be proved to the general satisfaction of all that history had been conned, would the knowledge make those plays any less outstanding?

What is a literary forger? Is he a criminal in the accepted sense of the word, or a misguided genius; an artist obsessed with personal greed, or a philanthropist? Money as a motivation is only part of the story—the last thing that would have occurred to Vaclav Hanka, a nineteenth-century Czech nationalist. Hanka, desperate to promote the traditions of Czech culture, overcompensated somewhat when he illuminated the famous fourteenth-century Jaromir bible. Unfortunately, as with most idealists, his enthusiasm was greater than his attention to detail. Nothing was wrong with his beautiful illustrations, but on the title page he printed 'Bohussus Lutomericensis Pinxit MCCLVIII'. One hears of writers and artists being ahead of their time, but never by precisely one hundred years!

The remarkable Thomas Chatterton (1760–77), one of the most romantic figures in English literature—described by the Irish critic and authority on Shakespeare, Edmund Malone, as the greatest genius England had produced since Shakespeare—could be just as careless. Chatterton's fertile imagination had created a medieval monk called Thomas Rowley and attributed to him a number of fascinating manuscripts he claimed to have found; in fact he had written them himself, in the contemporary poetic rhythm which ultimately earned him such high praise from nineteenth-century literary figures. But as a writer, the content was obviously more important to Chatterton than factual detail, and one book was entitled: *Battle of Hastings, wrote by Turgot the monk, a Saxon, in the tenth century and translated by Thomas Rowlie, parish prieste of St Johns in the city of Bristol in the year 1465*. For those readers educated outside Britain or France, perhaps I should add that the battle, perhaps the most famous date in British history, took place in 1066; that is, in the *eleventh* century.

With very early books and manuscripts, forgery was predominantly concerned with illustration, and the fourteenth century has proved an irresistible attraction to many. Another forger unconcerned with personal gain, or at least with financial gain, was the Italian painter Pietro Nanin, who at one time in the nineteenth century was president of the Academy in Verona. It was his obsession for the rare and beautiful that prompted him to adorn manuscripts and incunabula owned by the local Museo Civico with illustrations in the style of the fourteenth century.

Before leaving illustrators, another most spectacular story is one which took place in Germany in the nineteenth century. A collector, Heinrich Klemm, gathered an impressive collection of early printed works which he persuaded artists to illustrate in a medieval style. His collection, now in the Deutsches Museum fur Buch und Schrift, at Leipzig, included a forty-two-line Gutenberg Bible (printed between 1452 and 1455; the thirty-six-line version was printed between 1457 and 1459) to which he had added 143 fake miniatures to 136 genuine ones!

Usually an uncovered forgery loses its value overnight, but Thomas Wise (1859–1937), who faked editions and pamphlets written by most of the leading nineteenth-century authors, must be chuckling in that great bookshop in the sky over the post-exposure success of his efforts. Many of his forgeries subsequently fetched considerably more than the originals. A copy of *Sonnets* by 'EBB' (Elizabeth Barrett Browning), Reading, 1847 (in fact London, c1890), sold in 1976 as part of the estate of John Carter (the bibliographer who with Graham Pollard finally unmasked Wise in 1934), fetched £1,800. The book, bound in blue levant morocco by Zaehnsdorf in a velvet lined morocco box, had been presented to Carter as a wedding present in 1937 by George Schlieffelin of Scribners. Carter's ownership undoubtedly had much to do with the price paid, but nine years before another copy had fetched £700. Such is their potential value that there have even been forgeries of the forgeries!

Wise, who was never criminally charged, and who died apparently without remorse three years after the publication of Carter & Pollard's *An Enquiry into the Nature of Certain 19th Century Pamphlets,* was a clever man capable of earning good money through legitimate channels. Such was his scholarship as a bibliographer specialising in nineteenth-century novelists that he was appointed President of the Bibliographical Society in 1922, and received an honorary Fellowship at Oxford two years later. His motivation for resolving to forgery was undoubtedly greed.

It has been said that his interest in literature sprang from his late childhood, when he would read poetry to an invalid mother.

As a young clerk he spent all his spare money on collecting although, as his knowledge grew, particularly of prices, he was able to buy and sell, which is how many collectors have graduated to bookselling. But Wise ostensibly remained a collector, pursuing his passion with such single-mindedness and shrewdness that he gradually amassed an impressive library, largely of first editions.

One of his early ploys was to trace the descendants and friends of famous writers and, by ingratiating himself, to buy from them at bargain prices (although it should be said in fairness to Wise that he was never afraid to pay handsomely for what he considered a choice item). Through this ability to deal from the 'inside' he had a tremendous advantage over other collectors and book sellers.

John Edward Trelawny, for example, little known today, was a close friend of Byron and Shelley, and, as the last survivor of that brilliant group, was buried by the side of Shelley in 1881. From Trelawny's son-in-law, Wise was able to pick up a copy of the suppressed *Oedipus Tyrannus* of Sophocles for about thirty pounds—no idle investment, because only a few years later another copy was sold for over £1,200.

This dedication, and subsequent success, probably explains why Thomas Wise had such an easy transition into dishonesty. One must bear in mind that he had the benefit of starting from a position of extreme respectability, having not only established himself as an authority on nineteenth-century writers but having also made a lot of money, cunningly but within the limits of legality, in the process. He had no need of money, so it must have been only greed that prompted him to overstep the mark.

By now he had added Robert Browning to the distinguished list of authors on whose works he was an acknowledged expert, a list including Byron and Shelley as well as Swinburne. In the 1880s Wise had become secretary of the Browning Society, of which he was a founder member, and before long he met the author. When he purchased from a bookshop the author's first published work, *Pauline* (1883)—which had originally flopped— at what ostensibly appeared an exorbitant price, Browning is said to have dropped him a postcard with the words 'Thanks, unwise

Wise'. Wise, on the contrary, knew what he was doing, and subsequently saw the value shoot up to 135 times what he had paid.

As an expert, he was called in to advise on the Swinburne library shortly after the poet's death in 1909, and took the opportunity to buy it for himself for £3,000. From there, not only did he sell many of the books and manuscripts for a profit, he also persuaded William Heinemann to pay him £900 for the publishing rights to some previously unpublished material which, considering it consisted mainly of work Swinburne had put on one side as sub-standard, was quite a lot of money for that time.

Meanwhile, Wise had persuaded the Browning Society to reprint *Pauline*, since the original had been privately printed by Browning at the age of twenty-one in a very limited run, and had not sold. Now that Browning was a success, Wise realised there would be a demand for his first work. (The style of that poem had apparently been heavily influenced by Shelley, and presumably did not blend easily with Browning's individualistic talent. Significantly, after this early disappointment, he changed to what in due course became easily identifiable as his own characteristic style.) Wise managed to get himself appointed editor, and decided to follow the original production closely, including the type, so that—by a strange coincidence—the reprint turned out to be an exact copy of the first edition. Nothing really wrong so far, since 400 copies had been approved as facsimiles by the Browning Society for sale to members; but how many copies were actually sold to members was never clear. What *is* known is that Wise was selling 'reprints' in 1910, long after the Society had been disbanded, while in the interim period a surprising number of first editions appeared on the market.

Concurrent with his involvement in the Browning Society, Wise was called in by the newly formed Shelley Society, and the same facsimile switch was tried again with three Shelley titles, to be followed by his first brazen dishonesty: the publication of *Poems and Sonnets*, by Percy Bysshe Shelley, limited to thirty copies, edited by Charles Alfred Seymour of the Philadelphia Historical Society. Editor and Society did not exist.

Like a bank-note forger, Wise would release his fake first

editions intermittently to avoid arousing suspicion. A twenty-year friendship with the American collector John H. Wrenn brought him a sinecure in return for the opportunity to offload practically every forged first edition he had ever attempted, and this extended not only to the authors already mentioned, but also to Lord Tennyson, John Ruskin, Robert Louis Stevenson, William Morris, George Eliot, W. M. Thackeray and Joseph Conrad. Apart from the forgeries, he also made huge profits on the sale of miscellaneous books to his trusting friend—and remember, in all this time Wise was never a bookseller, and actually denied such charges with indignation.

In 1903 the editors of a bibliography of Ruskin's works (Cook and Wedderburn) cast serious doubts on the authenticity of certain Ruskin items drawn to their attention by Wise: but such was his rock-like façade of respectability that he slipped off the hook without undue embarrassment. Then, in 1920 a Swinburne bibliography by Flora Livingston, a librarian at Harvard University, asked further questions about the integrity of Wise, and seven years later her bibliography of Rudyard Kipling renewed the attack. By now Wise had gone 'straight', concentrating on genuine bibliographical works, and it was in this period that he received his literary honours. But the evidence against him, accumulated over the years, was examined afresh by Carter and Pollard and their detective work eventually paid dividends.

One should bear in mind that the professional forger undertaking the reproduction of a rare incunabula faces a monumental task. And, although the potential reward might seem enormous, in the main he is more likely to be restrained by the difficulty of finding buyers. There are undoubtedly easier ways of making a living! If he really must do something illegal it would be far simpler if he lowered his horizons.

On the face of it, Thomas Wise was not taking much of a risk. Because of his passionate interest in the nineteenth century and his authority acquired through a genuine knowledge, he did not have far to look for his subjects. One would also have thought that he could have avoided the print and production problems facing the man working on a medieval manuscript. One would have been wrong.

Whether it arose through overconfidence, or (uncharacteristically) plain stupidity, it was precisely such a technicality that pulled the rug from under his feet. Carter and Pollard discovered that certain Wise books which might be fakes were at Hodgson's Saleroom, coming up for auction. Taking J. G. Millward, the experienced sales clerk, into their confidence, they persuaded him to allow them to cut a strip less than one thirty-second of an inch (about 0·75mm) wide off the edge of one page to send for analysis. The report revealed that the paper contained wood pulp and esparto grass, which were not in use at the time of alleged publication. Further tests indicated that the typeface was also too modern, and typographical examination of other Browning and Shelley pamphlets with 'early' dates proved that they also had been printed after 1880. To cap it all, Carter and Pollard discovered that none of the vast number of suspected forgeries had actually appeared on the literary scene before 1888.

Without attempting to list the technical problems, it is as well for the collector reading this to know some of the more significant stages in the development of book production, if only to assist him in dating the rare volumes he might discover from time to time. As I said earlier, printing was not invented by Gutenberg and Caxton; the ability to cast type with few restrictions merely opened the floodgates. Tracing the earliest roots of printing, one has to go back to the days of the Greeks and Romans, who used a form of stamp, while the Chinese and Koreans worked with engraved metal signets. The next breakthrough was a movable type known to have been used by the Chinese in the thirteenth century, although even before that the Japanese were experimenting with block printing—to which, ironically, the Chinese reverted because of the multiplicity of the characters required; in consequence more than three hundred years were to elapse before the Chinese 'rediscovered' movable type from Europe.

Yet, although letterpress and lithograph techniques have obviously become very much more sophisticated in the five-hundred years since the days of the first hand-presses, the fundamentals remain the same. All this means that even an enthusiastic amateur could probably find an old printing press which could be adapted to his needs. The greater headaches lie in obtaining suitable materials, particularly paper and inks.

Once again, it was the Chinese, in AD 105, who made the first giant stride towards what we know today as paper, although the papyrus of Egypt provided a platform for that breakthrough. 'Papyrus' (in Greek *'papuros'* from which we get the modern 'paper') is a long, aquatic reed-like plant from which, in ancient Egypt, strips were cut, pressed together, dried in the sun and glued into a roll. The earliest preserved written papyri date back to the first half of the third millenium BC. Papyrus was displaced by parchment and vellum by the fourth century AD, but continued to be used in the Middle East for documents and private letters until the eleventh century. (Parchment was prepared from the skin of a sheep or domestic animal, soaked in lime, stretched, and then scraped and polished. Vellum, prepared from the skin of calves, is the finer article.)

What the Chinese did was to break plants down into the original fibres by beating them before forming the fine strands into a web or sheet. The principle was copied by the Arabs in the eighth century and developed by them in their travels, coming to Europe *via* their conquests in Spain. In the eleventh century the knowledge was passed to Italy and subsequently to Germany and France, from which it came to England. There are no very early records of paper manufacture in England—possibly the first being contained in a poem in 1490 by William Vallans called *A Tale of Two Swans* in which he referred to a paper mill at Hertford. Five years later Caxton printed Wynkyn de Worde's *De Proprietatibus Rerum* which mentioned John Tate's mill, believed to be the same one.

Paper was still being made by hand from rags soaked in water and bleach and crushed to a fibrous state in a pulp vat. A woven cloth would be stretched tightly across a frame the size of the required sheet of paper; another frame was then placed on top of this mould and the whole thing dipped into the vat containing the wet mixture. When the pulp had been spread evenly across the cloth area, the outer frame was removed and the fresh 'paper' removed and placed between alternate layers of paper and felt, to be pressed and dried. When dry it was coated with animal-based size to provide a writing surface and prevent the ink penetrating too far, and glazed by rolling between sheets of polished zinc.

In 1799 the first machine for producing a continuous web of paper was introduced. Shortly after, resin size replaced animal glue, and the next important milestone was the introduction of wood pulp, as an alternative to rags, in 1840. With a little practice you should be able to examine the constitution of paper in books from your collection and tell the difference between those published before the beginning of the nineteenth century (the demarcation period between hand-dipped and machine-made paper, and between the different glues) and those published after 1840, when wood pulp was introduced.

With early printed books, the forger also had to contend with watermarks. Fortunately—or unfortunately, depending on your point of view—because the changes in paper composition between the fifteenth and sixteenth centuries were slight, one can fake a watermark or, where possible, use the unprinted fly-leaves and endpapers of genuine early books which have no special significance. William Ireland, who had a brave try at forging Shakespeare, managed to acquire these in some quantities, as well as cutting off the ends of old rent rolls. But, even though watermarks can be faked in three or four effective ways, the difference can be detected under microscopic examination or by chemical testing—although this latter process has to be conducted with extreme caution, whether examining the watermark or the paper itself, because of the damage that can be caused. Furthermore, since records exist for every known watermark from 1282 to the beginning of the seventeenth century, experts (and this includes collectors specialising in incunabula) can often distinguish between genuine and fake by appearance alone.

Because of such difficulties, even the forger going for the jackpot would never attempt a complete work but would try his hand instead at a single page of something in exceptional demand—a Gutenberg Bible, for example. But, at the prices involved, nobody accepts newly discovered items, no matter how ingeniously 'planted', at their face value! So, today, life at the top in book forgery is hard. In the days before scientific methods of detection the forger having to contend only with 'expert' opinion, had at least a sporting chance.

However, fate has seldom been kind to such tricksters, many of whom had exceptional literary talent in their own right; had they had the 'advantages' modern writers enjoy—with the support of a literary agent, for example—they might have been revered names today. One could not find a greater contrast to Wise than Thomas Chatterton, who, in addition to Malone's praise, was hailed by the critic Edmund Gosse a hundred years later as 'the most extraordinary phenomenon of infancy in the literature of the world', and by Walter Watts-Dunton as 'The Renascence of Wonder Incarnate'. Chatterton's story is dramatic enough to have inspired many artists and writers to honour him. Among them were poets of the Romantic Revival, Coleridge, Shelley, Keats, and Wordsworth, who called him 'that marvellous boy, the sleepless soul that perished in his pride'. There are more than twenty books on Chatterton and his works.

The pride to which Wordsworth referred caused a seventeen-year-old Chatterton to take arsenic at his lodgings in London, having lived for several weeks on the verge of starvation. Those who do not know his tragic story are advised to correct their oversight,* but in this bare outline it is sufficient to say that his obsessive interest in the past lasted a mere ten years, beginning at the age of seven when he found an old Bible (which he used to teach himself to write), an age when his favourite recreation was reading inscriptions on gravestones in the old local churchyard. He was unable to share the interest (his main preoccupation being with the fifteenth century) with anyone at home or at school, and he became more and more withdrawn, spending every spare moment studying the past and its language. But his literary skills were already developed, and, when he was eleven, a satirical poem he wrote about vandalism at his church was published by a local newspaper.

Eventually Chatterton befriended a young teacher at the school and, to impress him, or perhaps just to give him pleasure, pro-

* See the selective bibliography at the end of this book.

duced a number of parchment manuscripts purportedly written
by the priest Thomas Rowley, probably based on a real character,
who had lived in fifteenth-century Bristol. By now completely
familiar with the vocabulary and style of the period (although he
occasionally made mistakes in translation when producing Anglo-
Saxon history 'transcribed' by Rowley), Chatterton turned out
poetry and verse with little effort, bringing to the works his
instinctive grasp of rhyme and metre. For paper he was able to
make use of genuine documents and manuscripts found by his
father in a chest at St Mary Redcliffe church, and never apparently
formally collated. All Chatterton then had to do was to erase any
contemporary writing—although, in view of his fascination with
the originals, he must first have read and practically memorised
every line. This genuine source also provided a convenient excuse
for 'discovering' the forged Rowley manuscripts.

After several of his own talented pieces were accepted by
different magazines, he sent *The Ryse of Peynctynge in England* (a
history of painting), by 'Thomas Rowlie', to Horace Walpole
whose *Castle of Otranto* (1765), usually considered to be the first
of the Gothic novels, was said to have been based on an old
manuscript he had found and translated. Walpole was not just
another writer in this particularly affluent period in English
literature; he was an important figure in society, being the son
of the distinguished Sir Robert Walpole, Minister to George II,
and he was a well known collector of art and curios of the past.
It was the interest in history and old manuscripts, and the fact
that Walpole had his own printing press, that prompted the
young man to try to sell him newly discovered fifteenth-century
manuscripts. By now a number had been published, but invariably
under a pseudonym.

Initially Walpole was impressed but, after calling on other
expert opinions, he became sceptical and eventually disinterested.
Chatterton was desperately short of money (even when his own
writing was in demand, editors somehow managed to avoid
paying), and his persistence probably antagonised Walpole,
who behaved shabbily, 'forgetting' to return the manuscripts
despite the young man's obvious agitation. It is generally considered that his callous behaviour was a major contribution to the

youth's eventual suicide; ironically, years later, in expressing his regrets, Walpole too conceded Chatterton's literary genius.

One wonders what might have happened if Chatterton had been a little more devious and produced his 'Rowley' stories under his own name, claiming merely to have based them on some old manuscript but without pressing the point. Walpole, after all, had made such a claim for *Otranto* and no one doubted his word— or cared much—although it must be admitted that Walpole was already an established literary figure. But the whole question of what is acceptable as 'borrowed' material, and when it becomes dishonest to use someone else's name (someone inevitably less talented), has always been a vexed one.

I have in my possession an interesting but innocuous little Victorian adventure story entitled *For God and Gold* (Macmillan, 1887) by Julian Corbett which has a second title-page reading:

FOR GOD AND GOLD
Calling on this ailing age to Eschew The Sins Imitate the virtues of
MR. JASPER FESTING
Sometime Fellow of Trinity College in Cambridge, and late an Officer in Her Majesty's Sea-Service
By This Showing Forth of
Certain noteworthy passages from his life in the said University and elsewhere, and especially his connection with the beginning of
The Puritan Party
Together with a particular relation of his Voyage to
Nombre de Dios
Under that renowned navigator
The late
Sir Francis Drake, Knight
written by himself
and now first set forth

In his preface, Corbett devotes three pages to pledge the authenticity of Festing's memoirs, a dissertation earnest enough for me to subsequently waste several hours of my time trying to trace the existence of the young seaman (later Macmillan reported that their records did not go back that far). I stopped searching when I realised how little it mattered. Corbett tells a good yarn and, whether he merely elaborated on known sixteenth-century history or followed the outline of someone else's manuscript, is immaterial. An original 'Festing' manuscript is another matter!

The same applies to a book still much in demand today, and in terms of sales over the years practically in the best seller category: Rudolf Raspe's *Narrative of Baron Munchausen*, first published in 1785, and a literary caper which got out of hand. A German, well educated but something of a scoundrel (he fled to England, suspected of having stolen certain valuable antique jewels and coins in his care), Raspe bursts in on the literary scene with an account of the larger-than-life but true story of an eighteenth-century soldier and adventurer, Freiherr von Munchausen. Raspe's vivid imagination embellished the rather fantastic stories to such proportions that they resembled fiction more than fact. But the book was such an instant success that other shrewd writers and editors added and subtracted episodes to such an extent that most versions read today indicate that von Munchausen is common literary property.

While I would hate to perpetuate the myth of 'fantasy' novels influencing the behaviour patterns of young people, it is a fact that sales of *Munchausen* were at their peak when William Henry Ireland (1777–1835) was in his impressionable teens. Whether it was innocent high spirits or a streak of maliciousness that prompted him to play the initial trick, on his own father, that was to have such devastating repercussions, we do not know. An apprentice, the lad was obviously bored with life and set out to liven things up, by 'discovering' an item of Shakespeariana. Unfortunately, like most practical jokes, his misfired, and the powder burns were suffered by his innocent victim. His father Samuel, an engraver with artistic and literary aspirations, who had become something of an authority on Shakespeare (later to prove his Achilles' heel), endured considerable humiliation and shame as a result of his son's deception; ultimately there was a rift between father and son which William's belated expressions of contrition could not mend. A single joke, is one thing; but William developed the theme with elaborate forgery and that required considerable time and effort, not to mention skill.

William forged a number of documents and works purportedly belonging to Shakespeare, in whom he shared his father's interest. Claiming to have discovered them at the home of a mysterious gentleman of substance, a fictitious 'Mr H' (inviting the assumption that Mr H was a descendant of John Heming, to whom Shakespeare had bequeathed his papers), the young man produced a steady stream of documentation, including various deeds, a Protestant 'confession of faith' by the playwright, letters to Ann Hathaway, Southampton and others, a new 'improved' version of *King Lear*, *Vortigern and Rowena* (allegedly an undiscovered play about the early Welsh king), and *Henry II*. There was even a 'thank-you' letter from Elizabeth I to the Bard.

The run-of-the-mill documentation was accepted universally by scholars and literary figures alike, among them an appreciative Boswell, obviously something of a blind hero-worshipper. And, to give him credit, young Ireland was pretty thorough in his researches, both historically and in the execution of his work. For example, he started by finding a facsimile of a Shakespeare deed, tracing the signature until he was reasonably adept at copying. He learned from a printer friend just how to produce the right inks, and for paper and old seals he was able to find a handy supply at the solicitor's office where he worked.

However, as a dramatist—still only nineteen years old—he was less effective. *King Lear*, on which he was not too ambitious, began to raise doubts and *Vortigern* was therefore examined even more carefully. Unfortunately, he had made a rod for his own back by announcing the remarkable discovery before he had completed the manuscript, so that he was forced to finish it rather hurriedly. Its announcement had, after all, been something of a bombshell, and there was considerable competition among theatre managements to present it—the honour being won by the playwright Richard Brinsley Sheridan, proprietor of the Drury Lane theatre. The eyes of the literary world were now focused on Ireland and, on the eve of the first public performance, Edward Malone, the Shakespearian authority, published a damning review.

Even so, the day might have been saved because, although the verse was distinctly sub-standard Shakespeare, the leading rôles were played by the top stars of the day, Mrs Jordan (the King's mistress) and John Kemble, whose performances might have 'lifted' the dialogue sufficiently to pass muster. But Kemble, convinced by Malone's dissertation, took the law into his own hands by 'hamming' up his part—especially when delivering such lines as 'And when this solemn mockery is ended', to which the audience responded well.*

Because of the esteem in which his father was held as an antiquary, it was generally assumed that Ireland senior must be responsible for the forgery, rather than his nineteen-year-old son, who was not well educated and who had no known literary aspirations. In fact, when the conscience-stricken William admitted everything, no one (including his father) would believe him. Even after he had written his confession in *Authentic Account* (1796), people remained convinced that Samuel Ireland was the villain of the piece, and constantly harassed and ridiculed him. The old man made matters worse by perpetuating his defence of the authenticity of the Shakespeare material. Even after William's *Confessions* (1805) there were still attacks on Samuel's integrity. Perhaps this is why, while he missed out on the jackpot and alienated his father, William survived to eke out a living from more undemanding bits of writing, adapting, translating and bookselling.

Another forger whose reputation survived—despite violent attacks from certain critics—enough for him to be buried in Westminster Abbey, was the poet James Macpherson (1736–96), who in 1762 published *Fingal*, an epic poem in six books, and subsequently *Temora*, in eight books. He claimed these as translations into English from a third-century Gaelic poet Ossian, whose work he had found during his widespread searches in the highlands and Hebrides.

Tales of Celtic romance captured the imagination of the

* *This Solemn Mockery*, Arlington, 1973, is the title of a book on forgers by John Whitehead.

literary world throughout Europe, Scandinavia and Russia, at the outset of the Romantic Movement, and sold exceptionally well; this may be why Macpherson was denounced by certain critics, including Doctor Johnson, literary success so often being despised. But what he did was to use his talent as a poet and his deep knowledge of highland tradition to embellish ancient legends, the origins of which are cloaked in the same sort of mystery that surrounds the legends of King Arthur. It has been suggested that Macpherson might have admitted earlier to the authorship of the magnificent *Fingal* had he not been hoist by his own petard: it was his often violent quarrels with Dr Johnson over the authenticity of the works that made him dig his heels in. In some ways it might be said that Macpherson bought his respectability, including his burial place, but no one denies his talent as a poet.

We have come full circle and are left still with the fruitless argument about the respective merits of originator *versus* disciple, innovator *versus* master craftsman. Whether the legends represented the sum of different talents over many generations of folk poets, whether Macpherson made it all up, or whether even Ossian really *was* the original author, literature would have been poorer without *Fingal*.

A final note on 'genuine' authorship. Not so many years ago, the *New Statesman* ran a contest for short stories in the style of Graham Greene. Unknown to the magazine and the many dozens of literary aspirants confident of fooling the world with their immaculate 'Greene' style, Graham Greene himself decided to enter the competition. His submission was placed third.

7 Sale by Auction

With relatively few exceptions, the most valuable books, both collections and individual titles, are sold today by public auction, although the main buyers are booksellers, who frequently represent collectors or libraries. There are a number of reasons why sales are conducted in public, not least because the average person only knows the bookshop on the corner where the proprietor's knowledge of rare books might be little better than his own. There are fewer 'fairytale' stories in the book world of the dusty volume in the attic being discovered to be a priceless treasure than there are in the world of paintings, for example, but it does happen. *A Book of Hours*, brought to the Munich office of Sotheby Parke Bernet & Co was recognised there by an expert as an unrecorded Flemish work, *c.* 1510, by Horenbout & Bening, and later sold for a world record price for any manuscript of £370,000.

The reality is that for many years there has been an uneasy alliance between bookseller and auctioneer, based on common interest and convenience. Today the relationship is exacerbated by an understandable jealousy of the growing power of the larger auction houses, such as Sotheby's and Christies. Critics say, with some justification, that people do wrong to by-pass them; that their expertise is far greater, and that they can offer a team of knowledgeable and experienced people compared with the single specialist expert representing the auction room. This is why, they say, there is often such a disparity between the pre-sale estimated price and the figure actually attained, and why the estimated price has sometimes been lower than the reserve! They concede that many people believe they will get a fairer deal in open competition, and therefore even the critic is obliged to take his place in that market place.

But what does stick in their gullet is the tendency now for the auction house to discreetly compete as a retailer by offering investment advice; *what* to buy. This was brought home sharply just a few years ago when a British Railway pension fund so advised outbid a national library for a collection which morally belongs to the nation, and not to someone concerned principally with re-sale values. Occasionally the auction house even buys books speculatively for future re-sale, perhaps on the grounds that the reserve price had not been reached.

From my position on the fence, I would say there is no question that certain giants are getting very powerful; they present a threat to larger bookdealers but, equally, they provide an invaluable service. A bibliophile wishing to sell his collection will shop around at three or four of the dealers he considers most appropriate. The days have gone when any professional picks up incredible bargains for nothing; in more and more cases, bookshops have to compete in an 'open' market for anything reasonable, which means that generally they have to pay a fair price. But many people do not have the advantage of knowing which shop is likely to be interested, and find it more convenient to go to one 'centre' where they can feel safe.

In the 'good old days' when the demarcation line was not so blurred, when auctioneer and dealer ostensibly worked closely, even important auctions in the UK were frequently rigged by what is commonly known as 'The Ring'. It was not at all uncommon, particularly in the provinces, for auctions to be conducted at lightning speed to get rid of the 'outsiders'; the spoils were then divided up in a second private affair. Allegations were always difficult to prove and, despite a 1927 Act of Parliament which set out to eliminate rigging, there has only ever been one prosecution—and no conviction. Fortunately such practices have almost disappeared and the auction scene today is basically honest.

The auction room means different things to different people:

lifeblood to the professional dealer; an awesome spectacle to the novice buyer, frightened to breathe in case the movement of his shoulders be misrepresented; a source of amusement to students of human behaviour. The auctioneer, the man on the spot, is part of the tableau and we seldom see him as an individual, yet in failing to do so we ignore his very special talents. His skills are seldom directly related to the product he is selling, yet his expertise and experience are vital. The strain of conducting an important sale can reach nightmarish proportions. He might, for example, have to contend with one dealer's secret signal of 'left shoulder raised' to indicate 'up £100', another's 'right shoulder drooping' to mean exactly the same, a third's 'imperceptible shrug' signifying 'up £200'—the identical shrug from a fourth meaning 'I'm out'—a fifth's signal that he is bidding so long as he remains seated (or standing), and a sixth's 'mopped brow' indicating 'it's hot in here'! So a room full of twitching, agitated dealers—not to mention those twitching quite involuntarily for a variety of medical reasons—has caused even experienced auctioneers to knock down lots to the wrong bidder. Other secret signals include hat on or off, standing up, and removal of handkerchief from breast pocket.

Equally, without quite the same degree of pressure, even experienced booksellers have purchased the wrong lot. Quaritch, for example, from their place at the very top of the tree, are not ashamed to admit that these things happen; they once triumphantly made off with some Greek manuscripts instead of the Icelandic sagas they had intended to buy. The confusion arose because, in the catalogue, the long description about the Greek lot ran into the description of the item they wanted. Fortunately, the 'unwanted' manuscript was taken off their hands almost immediately by a library which had missed the sale.

It might seem surprising that, with the acute shortage of 'good' antiquarian material, the average bookseller still manages to pick up some of the items he wants, despite competition from more affluent rivals. The reason is that most still have specialist interests; if I happen to deal in a field as narrow as, say, bedpans of the sixteenth and seventeenth centuries, I could usually justify spending more on a desirable item than the general bookseller.

Nor does it necessarily follow that the man with the most money always wins (admittedly, he seldom loses), because of a variety of other considerations. A dealer buying for re-sale, for example, is perhaps conscious of his rising overheads and the headaches of further investment; that is, tying up cash without the promise of an early return. If he is representing a collector or institution on a ten-per-cent commission (supposedly a standard fee, but frequently knocked down by the client) he may be worse off than if buying for himself with various customers in mind. Such commissions are often an embarrassment; they are awkward to refuse, yet, except in the cases of very expensive lots, not very lucrative given the work involved—which can entail a personal inspection of the book and research into its antecedents and general background. This work might end in a recommendation *not* to buy; in that case, valuable time remains unpaid for.

From the spectator's point of view, a battle between dealers refusing to concede can be stirring—as a result of his battles Bernard Quaritch came to be known as the Napoleon of the auction room. These days, when the sky seems to be the limit, the chances are that the contestants are bidding for a rich collector or library. The irony is that on occasion dealers, in the interests of their clients, have dropped out when they considered the price had soared to an 'outrageous' level—only to be reprimanded by the unappreciative client who really did mean '*any* price'. One West End firm, asked by a South American millionaire to get a travel book (which they considered worth a few hundred pounds, although it might fetch more) at any price, did eventually purchase it for thousands of pounds, after getting involved in a bidding duel with someone who had a similar brief. Having spent considerably more than the book was worth, they were informed that their client had been seriously hurt in a car smash. He recovered sufficiently to pay for the book but, while the firm applied on his behalf for an export licence, he died. The book stayed in their safe until, much later, the man's wife took delivery. With no interest in her husband's purchase, the widow put it up for auction in New York where, of course, it fetched only a fraction of the price! Inevitably, money indiscriminately spent distorts prices at auction. Booksellers acting for a client will

'Modern' binding for Shakespeare's *Hamlet*, illustrated by Edward Gordon Craig, and printed on vellum at the Cranach Press, Weimar, 1930. The binding by Philip Smith is in black and grey scarf-joined Oasis moroccos with feathered onlays and 'maril' (marbled inlaid leather) invented and patented by the binder. The design is an expressive interpretation of the drama in psychological terms. The front board is divided geometrically along classical lines by the letters HAM above and LET (somewhat difficult to make out in this black and white reproduction) below, containing elements and incidents found in the play; e.g., the whole cover is the face of Hamlet, with the ship carrying the Prince of England as his 'eye' (which symbolises also Hamlet's moment of insight into the plot against him while on board ship). The group of figures carrying off the body of Hamlet form his mouth. The points of the crown, in which the letter A containing Ophelia (his conscience) strikes down like a ray of light from above, metamorphose across the covers into the towers and battlements of Elsinore castle. His father's ghost hovers between Heaven (the church quatrefoil window) and Hell (red flames) on the spine of the book, pointing to the inset depicting the pernicious usurping royal couple, with the mad Ophelia drowned below. Other details in the leather fragments are Yorick's skull, masks of the players, the poison goblet and the thorns of life.

A Sale at Sotheby's, by Thomas Rowlandson

The Fair Stationer in Hyde Park 1780

The Fair Stationer in Hyde Park, 1780; one of several scarce etchings of Hyde Park b
Paul Sandby. (*Courtesy of Baynton-Williams, booksellers and print specialists of Belgravia*

usually retain some sense of balance, but powerful men do not necessarily wish professional assistance in the saleroom, especially if they have a minion in the city concerned. Instructed to buy 'everything on page ten' the minion will blindly do so, which often means that an item going to him in the morning for a hundred pounds might have a duplicate or even better copy turning up in the afternoon for twenty pounds.

Not surprisingly, rival firms make the most of such 'clangers'; but the man who cannot afford to sneer is the auctioneer himself, who is seldom interested purely in selling at any cost. Apart from his reputation for integrity and complete impartiality, he is very much aware of the fact that his bread-and-butter trade depends on the goodwill of booksellers and collectors, who can only be rooked once. Obviously, in the interests of the vendor, he has to get the price as high as possible, while the bookseller does his best to get it as low as possible, but between those extremes there is considerable room for common sense. The rapport between auctioneer and bookseller is vital, especially as the former often has to hold bids for the latter—either in his unavoidable absence, or because he does not always want people to know he is bidding. Fred Snelling of Hodgson's once held bids from three specialists in sixteenth- and seventeenth-century English literature—each of whom thought his rivals were better informed, and was therefore reluctant to publicly announce his considered assessment of the lot's value. In such circumstances, incidentally, if bids of £50, £100 and £150 have been made, the auctioneer has to start with the second to preserve the anonymity of the contestants. (It does not follow, of course, that a man bidding £100 in such circumstances has to pay the full amount; he may be successful for only £10.)

The auction gradually became established toward the end of the seventeenth century, and it has come a long way in 300 years. The first of which there is any record in England was tried by a bookseller called Cooper in 1676, when he prefixed his catalogue with:

Reader, it hath not been usual here in England to make sale of books by the way of auction, or who will give most for them;

but it having been practised in other countries, to the great advantage of both buyers and sellers, it was therefore conceived (for the encouragement of learning) to publish the sale of those books in this manner of way.

The idea spread to the Provinces and, particularly successfully, to Dublin. A leading auctioneer, Edward Millington, quickly became known for his style and wit. It was he who rounded on his audience with the words: 'Who but a sot or a blockhead would have money in his pocket, and starve his brains?' Since at that time bids of one (old) penny were commonly made and accepted, we might sympathise with his somewhat aggressive approach.

Book auctions certainly created interest. Ralph Thoresby, in his *Diary*, describes what he says was the first ever held in Leeds, on 7 January 1693:

The large chamber, being overcrowded with the press of people, in an instant sunk down about a foot at one end; the main beam breaking gave so terrible a thunder-like crack, and the floor yielding below their feet, the people set up such a hideous noise, apprehending the fall of the whole house, at least the sinking of the room (which, in all probability, had been the death of most present), as was most doleful and astonishing, though I, sitting upon the long table by the books was at first not apprehensive of the danger; but being informed, I hasted out with what expedition I could.

Thoresby does not describe the books for sale, or what happened to them, but someone smarter than the rest probably stayed on to pick up some bargains.

Since most of the auction-room headlines are made through the sale of enormously expensive art treasures, it is soldom realised that Sotheby's, the biggest of them all, were book specialists for many years after their founding in 1744—two years before their main rival Christie's.

Samuel Baker, who little imagined his firm would, some 230 years later, be turning over more than £8 million a year in books and manuscripts, began very simply with the sale in January

1744 of Doctor Thomas Pellet's library. But he and his successors had a knack for attracting important material and the collections of many distinguished names: for example, the manuscripts of the first Lord Clarendon, including his autographed draft of the *History of the Great Rebellion*; and the collections of Henry Fielding, Joseph Addison, Prince Talleyrand (realising £8,399, which was a fair sum in 1816), Napoleon (his books from St Helena), William IV, Robert Southey, William Beckford (auctioned over 40 days in 1882–3 to realise £73,552), and William Morris.

I keep coming back to Napoleon and his obsession with books, although I hardly need to apologise in view of the interest in him. At the sale in 1823 of his St Helena books—the quality of which indicated that he had lost his taste for cheap novels—more excitement was created by the inclusion in that library lot of his walking stick. Formed of one piece of tortoiseshell, with a musical head, the stick was snapped up for £38 17s (£38.85).

But Christies managed to upstage their rivals 146 years later (although they were far too gentlemanly to draw attention to the significant detail, what might be described as the object 'lost' in the small print) when they auctioned Napoleon's relics brought back from St Helena by his chaplain, L'Abbé Vignali.

Vignali, a Corsican priest sent by Cardinal Fesch (Napoleon's uncle) to establish a chapel on the island, stayed with the Emperor until his death. In his will, Napoleon left him 100,000 francs and also entrusted him with a number of objects from the chapel—mostly silver and gold vessels, altar cloths, and such—which Vignali was to take to Napoleon's son, the Duke of Reichstadt in Vienna. In fact, they never got there although, after a long, tortuous journey, the objects are today in the possession of a descendant, Prince Victor Napoleon. But, apart from these and other personal belongings willed to specific members of his entourage, there remained a number of objects divided between Vignali and his companions. It was Vignali's share that was auctioned in London in 1969. The most bizarre item in the collection, which included the Emperor's death mask and a number of documents and letters, was what the catalogue listed as:

A small dried-up object, genteely described as a mummified tendon, taken from his body during the post mortem. The authenticity of the macabre relic has been confirmed by the publication in the *Revue des Mondes* of a posthumous memoir by St. Denis, in which he expressly states that he and Vignali took away small pieces of Napoleon's corpse during the autopsy.

In terms of magnitude, the most fabulous collection ever auctioned has been the Bibliotheca Phillippica, which Sotheby's have been selling by instalments since 1886. The story of Sir Thomas and his obsession is told in the Chapter 1, and when one recalls that he set out to own a copy of every known early printed book—and made a pretty brave stab at it—you can take my word that one could devote an entire book to listing the innumerable treasures that have come under the hammer. Each auction has produced a series of breath-taking lots, fascinating for their stories and associations as well as for the vast sums of money involved. The sufferings of history, for example, are dulled by repetition and time, but personal accounts bring such events to life. The Dissolution of the Monasteries has become to many yet another 'statistic' to be absorbed in a study of a larger-than-life Henry VIII, yet it was an agonising period for the men wh devoted their lives to the Church. In the first of the STC (short-title catalogue) sales in 1973, for example, one item was a 1537 first edition of Matthew's version of the Bible which belonged to John Alcetur (Alcester), a monk at the great Benedictine Abbey of Evesham. The Abbey, partly owing to its size and partly to the resistance of Abbot Lichfield, was one of the last to be suppressed. Only about twenty Benedictine abbeys and priories survived into the year 1540, and by the end of that year not one remained. Alcester had made extensive annotations in Latin and English, and had covered three blank pages with a musical score, probably of his own composition. However, it is his personal record, at the end of the Book of Maccabees, of Henry's tough measures that makes poignant reading today. He wrote:

. . . the monastery of Evesham was suppressed by Kyng

Henry the viii the xxxi yere of his raygne the xxx day of Januer at Evensong tyme the convent beyng in the quere [choir] at thys verse [in the Magnificat] Deposuit potentes and wold not suffur them to make an ende. Phillypp Ballard beyng Abbot at that tyme and xxxv Relygius men at that day alyre in the seyde monastry . . .

It is thought that within two months of the suppression of the Abbey, Alcester's Bible was taken from him.

Another personal note, from a French schoolboy of the ninth or tenth century, is recorded on one of the world's oldest school textbooks, a manuscript copy of the *Ars Grammatica* by Aelius Donatus, the 'founder' of Latin grammar. Generations of schoolboys, through the Middle Ages and the early Renaissance, from Donatus' own pupil St Jerome down to Sir Thomas More, learned their Latin from his *Ars Minor* and *Ars Major*. Manuscripts of Donatus are exceptionally rare, and only one of the *Ars Major*, produced as late as the fifteenth century, is recorded. The schoolboy inscription reads: 'This book belongs to Sado. His mother gave it to him. Great honour to her who gave this book.'

In terms of antiquity, that was merely a second-hand bauble compared with the first lot in the tenth sale of Phillipps' medieval manuscripts (new series) in November 1975—an Egyptian papyrus, the *Book of the Dead of Nes-Khonsu*, 21st–22nd Dynasty (*c.* 1095–800 BC). The main accent of that particular sale, however, was on European manuscripts dating from the ninth century. Highlights include a fourteenth-century *Bestiary*—the only recorded German illustrated bestiary (eighty-six coloured drawings of animals, birds, reptiles, etc.)—from the Carthusian monastery of Salvatorberg. The price paid for this masterpiece was £60,000.

Another giant collection dispersed in nine sales between 1965 and 1975 was that of the late Major J. R. Abbey, including his Hornby manuscripts (Charles St John Hornby, founder of the Ashendene Press and for many years a partner in the firm of W. H. Smith), dating back to the eleventh to fifteenth centuries, which realised well over a million pounds. Quite obviously there were many dozens of incredible books and manuscripts put under the hammer over this period, but the Hornby manuscripts sold in 1974 and 1975 realised the most fantastic prices. In the first sale, for example, auction records were smashed in no uncertain fashion. A new York dealer, John Fleming, paid £42,000 for a twelfth-century *Glossed Minor Prophets* from the scriptorium of Anchin near Douai, which in 1933 fetched all of £560; £34,000 was reached for a fine French manuscript, the *Cauchon Hours* from Rheims (c. 1430), which had been sold for £1,850 in 1925.

The other gargantuan collection (in complete contrast, it comprised later colour-plate books) was the Arpad Plesch botanical library, probably the finest of its kind ever assembled privately. Plesch, a Hungarian, conceived the foundation, the *Stiftung fur Botanik* in Lichtenstein, as a repository for rare plants as well as rare books on the subject. Practically every authority and artist of distinction is represented in the collection, artists of the reputation of P. J. Redoute, of Belgium, considered one of the great botanical painters of all time. Sold in only four instalments, the library fetched £582,866, and this included such literary landmarks as John Martyne's *Historia Plantarum Rariorum* (1728–37), which was the first botanical work with colour printed plates (£5,200: November 1975); *The Vegetable System*, by the celebrated English botanist John Hill, twenty-six volumes published between 1759 and 1786, with 1,222 hand-coloured plates and sixteen uncoloured (£7,200: same sale); and Redoute's *Les Liliacées* (1802–6), in eight volumes, one of the great masterpieces of botanical illustration, limited in the original issue to 280 copies (£19,000: March 1976).

Sales at Hodgson's Rooms have tended to be rather less spectacular, but equally fascinating in subject matter. May 1974 saw the auction of a collection relating to Saint Bridget of Sweden, whose prophecies and mystical writings had such a profound effect on European religious and political thought at the time of the Reformation. Among forty-five incunabula was *St Bridget's Revelations*, the earliest extant Latin edition, printed for Vadstena Monastery before 1492 with fourteen full page woodcuts and thirteen large historiated initials, some hand-coloured; it was purchased by Martin Breslauer, before he went to New York, for

£11,000. (I was intrigued to note from the records that a couple of the lots sold—in a total sale figure of £74,000, the highest for a single sale reached at Hodgson's since sales were first held there—went to, appropriately enough, a Mr Hammer!)

Hodgson's, although founded as late as 1807, is actually London's oldest book saleroom, having been at its present premises in Chancery Lane, off Fleet Street, since 1863. The building was actually designed for the purpose, and today remains basically unaltered; the rostrum, still in use, is surely one of the oldest in the world. The company was taken over by Sotheby's in 1967, and today book sales are divided between Bond Street and Chancery Lane, with the latter specialising in children's books, illustrated books of the nineteenth and twentieth century and modern first editions (from 1880). Other categories include law books of all periods, since the premises lie between two of the Inns of Court (Temple and Lincoln's Inn); this has given Hodgson's a tradition to maintain, following such milestones as the sale of the library of the College of Advocates in 1861, which took eight days.

Although certain purists will accuse me of vulgarity for thinking in terms of records, I am sure most readers will share my weakness for drama. The highspot was the £370,000 paid in Munich for the *Hours of the Virgin*, illuminated by Horenbout and Benning (*c.* 1510), especially dramatic since the owner did not know its value . . . and a long haul from the ten guineas paid in 1775 for the first western medieval manuscript to be sold by the firm, a tenth-century Greek Gospel in two volumes.

At Zurich in 1975, Sotheby's sold the David Sassoon historic collection of thirty-eight Hebrew and Samaritan manuscripts, one of the world's outstanding Jewish libraries, for over one million pounds. In some ways the Sassoon family is almost as fascinating as the collection. David Soloman Sassoon (1822–1942) was one of the many grandsons of the David Sassoon who moved from Baghdad to Bombay in 1832 and there laid the foundations of an incredible mercantile and banking empire which stretched from India to Hong Kong and Western Europe. Various members of the family distinguished themselves internationally in banking, commerce, industry and politics; one was the English poet and writer, Siegfried Sassoon. Among the exceptionally rare items sold was the Damascus Pentateuch, written in the Babylonian square of the ninth century—probably the oldest manuscript in existence, containing a large portion of the Bible in Hebrew, although fragments of older rolls and codices survive among the Dead Sea Scrolls in papyrus, and in fragments of the Cairo Genizah.

Early Arabic material is always much in demand, and more recently a single manuscript, a fine Quran written by the scribe Yagut al-Musta'simi—sometimes called 'The Sultan of Calligraphers'—in Baghdad in 1282, was bought for £62,000. Part of the illumination is contemporary with the manuscript and the rest was done in the sixteenth or early seventeenth century.

Parke Bernet, of New York, taken over by Sotheby's in 1975, also has its share of world auction records, for autograph material (George Washington's corresponsdence on his Mount Vernon estates, $250,000), for modern first editions (Kipling, *The Smith Administration*, $10,000) and for photographic material (Curtis, *The North American Indian*, $60,000). When Christie's followed their rivals to New York the auction scene became very much more competitive and exciting, with, before long, the giants having to look to their laurels from the fresh challenge of another 'export', Phillips, as well as old established American houses such as the Swann Galleries. Christie's New York hold the world auction record of £216,393 for a printed book, an Audubon *Birds of America*.

In contrast to the world of very intense competition and constant record-breaking, there are still a few outposts of relative tranquillity where the atmosphere has changed little in the past two hundred years. B. G. Grant Uden, a book collector of considerable experience who retired early from his post with the Ministry of Education to write on history, suddenly found himself pitchforked into this strange new world when, in 1968, he was asked to advise a Somerset auction house on what they recognised merely as a miscellaneous collection of bookplates. The firm, T. R. G. Lawrence of Crewkerne, for whom he soon became full time consultant, had until that time had little to do with books—so the name Audubon did not mean much!

The untidy bundle of colour plates found in an attic were recognised by Grant Uden as 42 of the original 435 hand-coloured plates, and the lot realised £5,400 which, at the time, was a record for such a small collection. But Grant Uden quickly discovered that although Crewkerne and the surrounding countryside were quite idyllic, not everyone shared his love of books. On a visit to a member of the local landed aristocracy (a well-known West Country landowner and eighth baronet), he was shown a basement full of seventeenth- and eighteenth-century calf-bound books, covered with mould, and in varied stages of decomposition. The books, hundreds remaining from what had once been a proud family library, had been left to rot. But, as an afterthought, the owner—who had thrown piles of others down a well, presumably because he could not get anyone to take them away—asked if there was anything saleable. Grant Uden dried and cleaned up what he could, and set to work with British Museum leather-dressing until some of the volumes were looking quite spruce. One of those thus salvaged was a good copy of the Duke of Newcastle's *General System of Horsemanship in all its Branches.* Having warmed towards his bibliophile benefactor, the baronet later added the final twist of the knife: 'I only put a few down the well. My father used a hell of a lot more to dam up the river when it burst its banks!'

Lawrence's first real influx of overseas bidders was in 1971, when the firm held probably one of the most fascinating literary sales of all time. Big guns of the antiquarian world, such as L. D. Feldman of New York (the man whose enthusiasm ruled his head in the battle to secure the *Alice in Wonderland* first edition, and who had a reputation for never accepting defeat), took the first 'crack-of-dawn' train from London. The draw was a collection inherited by the Ornithological Institute of letters and manuscripts written to and by C. K. Ogden while he was editing *The Cambridge Magazine,* 1912–22; he became a bibliophile later in life. The manuscripts and letters kept during his editorship represent one of the most important collections of English literary talent of the period ever assembled. The material was auctioned in individual lots each of one or two items, so that the individual prices realised were not especially staggering, but practically everything had a story. Apart from many interesting letters written by his contributors to Ogden there were also a number of unpublished poems—by, for example, Rupert Brooke, Edmund Blunden, John Masefield, Harold Munro, John Galsworthy, Robert Graves, W. H. Davies, A. E. Houseman, John Drinkwater, Ezra Pound, Edith and Sacheverell Sitwell, Siegfried Sassoon and James Joyce. Feldman's long journey proved worthwhile since he snapped up most of the 'plums'.

Because of Grant Uden's special interests and experience, Lawrence's of Crewkerne have gained a reputation in the sale of autographs and manuscripts (personal, as opposed to classic). One of these highlights was a collection of letters from Cassandra, sister of Jane Austen, which included references to the items in her will and mention of Jane's possessions, such as the ring with her hair set in pearls, always worn by Cassandra. The letters were bought by a leading London autograph specialist, Winifred Myers.

But a few years later it was an anonymous buyer who outbid the world's leading specialist dealers to acquire (at Sotheby's) the autograph manuscripts of two of Jane Austen's early novels, *Evelyn*, and *Catherine, or the Bower* for £30,000 plus the buyer's ten-per-cent premium. The first Austen manuscript to be auctioned in thirty years, and one of only eight that survive, the lot consisted of a vellum-bordered notebook covered in faded brown lines of Jane Austen's even italic script, and signed by her on the contents page 'May 6, 1792'. Ironically, on the same day, another lot, autograph poems by William Morris, failed to reach its reserve price.

The Jane Austen price, however, is by no means a record, an 'honour' received six months earlier by the autograph manuscript of Lord Byron's poem *Beppo*, which reached £50,000. Of course, even this figure would pale into insignificance by the side of anything that one could attribute to Shakespeare. But, apart from fabricated versions from the pen of William Ireland, nothing has ever emerged and probably nothing ever will. Meanwhile, we have to be content with a wealth of contemporary material, little of which is important.

However, in 1972, what has been described as the most important literary discovery of the century—an unknown play (*c*. 1611) by Thomas Heywood, a contemporary of Shakespeare, sold for £45,000. The play, a tragi-comedy unnamed because the flyleaf of the manuscript notebook is missing, is freely adapted from Richard Johnson's novel of 1599, *The Most Pleasant History of Tom a Lincolne, that Renowned soldier, the Red Rose Knight.*

The notebook was discovered at Melbourne Hall, Derbyshire, home of the Marquess of Lothian, among papers of Sir John Coke (1563–1644), Secretary of State, and although it is written in three different hands the research carried out by manuscript expert Peter Croft indicates that the play's author was Heywood. The principal reason for this conviction—despite the knowledge that one of the writers was a Morgan Evans, who has added notes on blank leaves at the end claiming that the notebook was his—is the existence of Heywood's distinctive vocabulary and dramatic technique, in relation to his known plays, *The Rape of Lucrece* and *The Four Ages*, and the frequent references to his native Lincolnshire. This is supported by the fact that the manuscript has a provenance indicating that it comes from Gray's Inn, with which Heywood had close personal links, several of his published plays being dedicated to members of that 'noble Societie'. It is known that the professional theatre companies used to supply plays for performance at the Inns of Court on their special grand 'feast' nights during the Christmas season—Shakespeare's *Comedy of Errors* was produced at Gray's Inn in December 1594—and it is believed that this unknown Heywood play was performed there in 1611–13, when Heywood was at his peak, and when Morgan Evans probably copied much of it from the prompt-book into his notebook.

Elizabethan scholars consider that one of the most striking features of the Heywood plays of Shakespeare's lifetime is the way in which he borrows ideas from the Bard, although it must be conceded that Shakespeare was himself not always the most original of playwrights. The Melbourne Hall play is said to contain chunks of atmosphere which might have been lifted from *Henry IV*, *Hamlet*, *King Lear* and *The Winter's Tale*. In the last, for example, the personified figure of Time as Chorus has an important linking presence, and in Heywood's play the tone and manner of Time's speeches indicate that his play might have been inspired by the 1611 performance of *The Winter's Tale*, especially in view of the similar themes. The fact that the play escaped recognition for so long is attributed to the form in which it survived.

In the sixteenth and seventeenth centuries Shakespeare was not held in the same esteem as he was in later centuries. One of his early critics made the following snide remark in a book published in 1638, as a tribute to the memory of Ben Jonson,

> *That latine Hee reduced and could command,*
> *That which your Shakespeare scarce could understand . . .*

The comment is believed to be the work of Edmund Waller, a talented poet, possibly making his first appearance in print. This seems especially likely since Waller seems to have been a very unpleasant character. He came from a Royalist family which supported the Parliamentary cause, betraying this cause in turn in a plot to seize London for the King. He was exiled and went to stay with the Royal family. Eventually he crawled back to London, befriended and fawned upon Cromwell, and turned yet again when the Protector died. (The book, incidentally, was part of Biblithetheca Phillippica's 'English books before 1641' collection, sold in 1974.)

The modern stage and the theatregoers of tomorrow were the concern of Robin Howard, whose valuable library of early printed books was sold in 1976 to aid the Contemporary Dance Trust by many thousands of pounds. Before donating the library to the Trust, Howard's wish was that 'future generations will find the contemporary theatre as fascinating as the theatre of the past'. Much of the attention was taken by an extremely rare early Bible in the collection, but a large number of outstanding literary items understandably reached high prices: for example, first editions of Shakespeare's *The Second Part of Henrie the Fourth* (1600—only one copy recorded), which realised £14,000, *Poems* (1640), £16,500, and *Comedies, Histories and Tragedies* (first folio 1623), £15,000. The last had an interesting inscription on the free front endpaper: 'This original edition . . . was bought for me in London by the Revd. Thos. Wilson . . . I payd five Guineas in the year of our Lord, 1772 John Thos. Waller, Castletown.' Other highlights were Howard (Henry, Earl of Surrey), *Songes and Sonnettes* (1559), said to be 'the first collection of lyric poetry in modern English, and one of the most significant books in English literature', which fetched £16,000, and a number of books by Francis Bacon and Beaumont and Fletcher.

The performing arts were represented at a sale in Monaco in 1975 of the finest Russian library in private hands, some 2,000 volumes assembled by two great names in the world of ballet, Serge Diaghilev and Serge Lifar. The venue was artistically appropriate since the Russian Ballet performed regularly in Monte Carlo between 1911 and 1929, and it became the company's winter base. The library's range was huge, starting with the work of the first printers to operate in Moscow—Ivan Fedorov and Peter Mstislavetz—the *Apostal* (Acts and Epistles of the Apostles) of 1564, which might seem a little late in the day, but remember the printers had to devise their own Cyrillic alphabet type-faces; the publication, in fact, took them a year to produce (£6,200). By way of contrast, the collection included original works of all the major nineteenth-century Russian writers, a highlight of which was an autograph leaf of Pushkin's corrected text of *Eugene Onegin*, in addition to nine first editions of his works. Among the musical works was the autographed manuscript of the whole of the finale of Stravinsky's *Firebird Suite*, signed and dated 31 March 1915. This was an unknown version of the suite; Stravinsky produced three known ones—in 1911, 1919 and 1945, with hitherto no mention of the 1915 version, which fetched £9,700. There were also two autographed manuscripts by Ravel, one being part of his unpublished orchestration of Mussorgsky's unfinished opera *Khovantchina*. It seems that in January 1913 Diaghilev, being dissatisfied with Rimsky-Korsakov's completion of *Khovantchina*, commissioned Ravel and Stravinsky to produce a new version in collaboration; this was first performed the same year in Paris.

The Diaghilev-Lifar library also included works illustrating the influence of the court on what was published in Russia in the eighteenth century, among them several satirical journals and plays actually written by Catherine the Great (1729–96), which in some ways conflicts with the picture handed down of a brilliant

tough ruler and diplomat, with few outside interests other than
the opposite sex. Yet Catherine not only found time to corres-
pond with Voltaire but wrote, both in her own name and under
the *nom de plume* of Major-General Boltin.

The memory of a far less interesting predecessor, the Tsar
Boris Godunov, was revived at another auction, when one lot
was his own copy of *Gospels*, written in Church Slavonic between
1598 and 1600, and considered to be possibly the most beautiful
Russian illuminated manuscript ever to appear at an auction. Its
small size and exquisite workmanship suggests that it was
intended for royalty rather than for the church; it has a contemporary binding, embroidered with silver and coloured silk
threads to a floral design and metal plaques showing Christ and the
four Evangelists. Inside, each gospel is preceded by a full-page
miniature of the Evangelist. Background and details are in gold,
and the miniatures are enclosed in borders with foliate designs in
colour. There are very unusual protective taffeta 'windows' on
the page facing the miniatures. It sold for £13,000.

Whether or not the incredibly self-centred Godunov regarded his
Gospels as anything more than a pretty titbit, there can be little
doubt that one man who collected because he appreciated fine and
unusual things was the seventeenth-century diarist John Evelyn,
considered in certain authoritative circles to be the 'father' of the
modern library. Evelyn seems to have been a dry, earnest person
somewhat lacking in warmth and personality, but a man of
integrity, and with a mind even more inquisitive in serious affairs
than his friend Samuel Pepys, being a scholar and founder of the
Royal Society. But he was not a rich man, and a considerable
number of the 4,500 volumes in his library had belonged at one
time to his father-in-law, Sir Richard Browne, British Ambassador
to France when they first met in 1643.

The history of the Evelyn library, which paints a unique and
comprehensive picture of Restoration life and learning, came to
public attention in 1977 when it was announced that it would have
to be sold, partly to offset death duties incurred by the death of a
descendant, Jack Evelyn, who had inherited the position of
'tenant for life' of the collection. The books had, of course, been

in the Evelyn family for 300 years, although they had been on loan to the Christ Church Library, Oxford, since 1950. The family decided that, as there was no longer a single custodian to the collection, they would sell the books and retain the manuscripts. It was, of course, appreciated that the family had little option, but there was an immediate outcry for the Government to step in and prevent the books going, as they must, to the United States. One historian is quoted as saying: 'In intellectual terms, it is as great a blow to the National heritage as to sell off Stonehenge, megalith by megalith.' One might comment that this is a rather melodramatic statement in view of the vast number of historical treasures that had already been allowed to leave these shores, and will no doubt leave in the future. The Government, in any case, was at the time preoccupied with the more down-to-earth issues of industrial relations.

Accordingly, the library went on sale at Christies in instalments, with the first series confined to books printed before John Evelyn's death in 1706, including not only the nucleus formed by himself but also others of the same period added by later members of the family. Many were collected during his travels abroad, from such sources as the sale of the Cardinal Mazarin library in 1650.

Part 1, A–C, alone fetched £252,901, indicating that the final tally might be in excess of one million pounds. I have already mentioned the £18,000 paid by Charles Traylen for a 1661 New Testament translated into Algonquin Indian, but Traylen also paid the highest amount on the second day, £13,000 for one of eighteen religious and scientific works by Robert Boyle—*The Sceptical Chymist: Or Chymico-Physical Doubts and Paradoxes, touching the spagyrist's principles commonly call'd hypostatical* (1661). In every sale, of course, there are items which fascinate some and bore others, and one lot I feel most people would have found interesting was John Bulwer's *Chirologia: Or the Naturall Language of the Hand. Composed of the Speaking Motions, and Discoursing Gestures thereof. Whereunto is added Chironomia: or the Art of Manuall Rhetoricke* (1664). That sounds on the face of it, merely sign language for the deaf, but a catalogue note explains: 'illustration of contemporary theories of acting, the inspiration for the book, according to the author, coming from Francis Bacon'.

And, to make it even more intriguing, the six full-page engraved illustrations have such captions as (in this case accompanying twenty-four pictures relating gestures to the letters of the alphabet):

An Index to the following Alphabet
of naturall Geftures of the FINGERS

Which Geftures, befides their typicall fignifications, are fo ordered to ferve for privy cyphers for any fecret intimation.

As a bibliophile I find it hard to reconcile that such an incredibly fascinating book, complete with press mark in Evelyn's hand (a book he would have enjoyed and probably discussed at some length with Pepys, in view of the latter's love and knowledge of the theatre), should realise only £750 (admittedly for re-sale), when at a furniture sale shortly before an ebony cabinet purchased by Evelyn in Italy, and mentioned in his diary, was knocked down, also to a dealer, for £26,000. But then I suppose a furniture enthusiast would wonder why anyone would pay £750 for an old book not even encrusted with gold and precious jewels.

The whole subject of values—not the prices that can be attained, but what buyers actually think of the properties they may have battled so earnestly to win—is a complex one. One does not need to reflect on the collector's reaction in moments of triumph, but what of the dealer? Does he sit back, awed or even captivated by the rarity, beauty, associations or literary merit of the object he temporarily owns? Or does he regard it dispassionately as a business transaction, a speculative investment on which he wants a return as soon as possible? A respected bookseller, who seldom buys anything that he would not wish to own and therefore keep for a while, dwelt sadly on the Chatsworth sale held by Christies, at which an expensive fourteenth-century masterpiece was purchased by three dealers acting jointly, each apparently more anxious than the next to offload their 'hot' property as quickly as possible, for fear that they had misjudged the market and overpaid; people like that would possibly not even mind whether they were buying Evelyn's cabinet or his *Chirologia*, so long as they had a customer lined up. This is not a criticism; it is merely a reflection on people's attitudes and their values.

Lackington's 'Temple of the Muses', from a coloured aquatint, published April 1809. The shop with its impressive circular galleries was eventually destroyed by fire. (*Courtesy of Baynton-Williams*)

Westminster Hall, 'The First Day of Term'. Copper plate engraving designed by Gravelot and engraved by Mosley in about 1740 and published in 1797. At each side of the Hall are wooden stalls for the sale of books and prints, rented by publishers and booksellers. (*Courtesy of Baynton-Williams*)

'Irish Binding'. Coloured caricature designed by George Woodward and published in 1812 by Thomas Tegg. 'Irish' jokes haven't changed much in the past 160 years or so. (*Courtesy of Baynton-Williams*)

A man who would have been greatly admired by Evelyn was Nicolaus Copernicus (1473–1543), the founder of modern astronomy, relevant in this context since the most important copy of his *De Revolutionibus* was sold for £44,000 at Sotheby's in 1974 as part of the library of early science, navigation and travel books of Harrison D. Horblit. The book had belonged to Andreas Goldschmidt, called Aurifaber (1512–59), and is inscribed to him by Joachim Rheticus on 20 April 1543, a month prior to Copernicus' death. Rheticus was the great man's principal disciple (his initials are on the binding). Copernicus was dying when the book appeared and did not inscribe any copies himself, but Rheticus, who supervised the printing after having persuaded his master to finish the book, signed two other copies—one now in the Vatican library and the other in the library of Uppsala University. *De Revolutionibus* is, of course, the first publication of Copernicus' theory that the sun is at the centre of our planetary system. This copy is important because it has a long autographed poem on the front flyleaves by the classicist Joachim Camerarius and annotations by Rheticus (who went on to publish his own work on the subject) on the first twelve pages of text as well as his marks and deletions on the title page and others.

'Firsts' of any category attract attention. What is believed to be the first ghost story published in English is *The Haunted Castle and Bold Oliver*, found in a lot of twelve volumes of *The Cabinet of Instruction and Amusement*, published by John Fairburn in 1800, in an auction of children's books in London a few years ago. As any bibliophile will know, prices of children's books, especially those decorated by the better known artists, have soared in recent years, although as far back as 1926 John Bunyan's *A Book for Boys and Girls* (1688) realised £2,100 at a Hodgson's sale. In 1977 *Kate Greenaway's Album*, one of the rarest books ever produced by her in that it was never actually published (the suspicion is that she was not very keen on the finished result) and only eight copies were actually printed, fetched £1,300. The book was only 3½ inches square and contained 192 miniatures.

The number of occasions when something valuable is found by accident is obviously diminishing, but it does still happen. In a pile of papers, part of the ephemera and rubbish attached to one sale lot being processed, an expert at Sotheby's (there are over twenty in the book department these days) browsed conscientiously but with fading interest through an old exercise book, and found a poem beginning *Gather Ye Rose-Buds*. The 'old scribble' turned out to be the poet Robert Herrick's commonplace book. Herrick (1591–1674), famous for his lyrics of the countryside and rural customs (another of his very English lyrics is *Cherry Ripe*), is obviously more highly considered than one might first have imagined, and the commonplace book sold for £50,000. I am sure there is a lesson there somewhere, if only to hang on to one's old notebooks!

8 'Talismans and Spells'

I had problems deciding where to begin this chapter. The theme 'fine and rare' justifies a book in its own right, and indeed several have been written on the subject. The difficulty is that we all have our own ideas of what constitutes beauty, mostly preconceived, since very few of us are lucky enough ever to see great master-pieces such as the Gutenberg Bible. In collecting, few of us assign the same relative values to print and master printer, to binding, even to literary content, so the issue is inevitably a personal one.

I was impressed with one of the glossy bibliographies published in 1975, *Great Books and Book Collections* by Alan G. Thomas, an antiquarian bookseller of fifty years' experience; yet certain critics took it to task on what were surely minor issues, such as his not providing the exact size of certain important volumes. And, despite my own enjoyment, I nevertheless wondered occasionally why the author had left out one of my 'dream' books, or I asked myself: 'Surely *Y* was a greater book than *Z*?' To avoid such criticism, I am restricting my commentary on the subject to general issues, and to mapping the history, trends and developments of fine book production.

All new techniques in the Arts need a harmonious climate in which to flower, and although the Germans might claim to be the fathers of modern printing—the people who put the jigsaw together, so to speak—it was to Italy that they looked for encouragement and sponsorship. The Italian princes and nobility, for all their faults, provided the financial resources for most cultural activity in the Middle Ages, and not only were they ready and willing to patronise the influx of craftsmen from Germany, and the other countries that followed, they also had on hand an abundance of literary manuscripts ideal for copying. Venice, a powerful republic at the time, became the Mecca for printers, for solid commercial reasons as well as because of its influence on the Arts. It was a commercial centre, famous for its maritime success (at a time when transport by sea was cheap).

History compresses the technological hallmarks of industrial evolution into what later seem like 'overnight' events, but even though the early printers were swimming with the tide the currents were not always favourable. They found themselves in the middle of not only an aesthetic controversy—how could print compare with the great tradition of beautiful handwritten works?—but also a considerable social revolution. The gift of reading was being offered to the ordinary man, and this would ultimately change the world. Because of their authority and power, the libraries were distinctly unhappy at the threat of the multiplication of books. So printing did not present its pioneers with the same golden opportunities to mint money as Lord Thomson would claim for commercial television 500 years later.

Indeed, one of the greatest names in printing, Aldus (1450–1515), had a sign over his door in Venice reading: 'Whoever thou art, thou art earnestly requested by Aldus to state thy business briefly and to take thy departure promptly. In this way thou mayest be of service even as was Hercules to the weary Atlas, for this is a place of work for all who may enter.'

The Aldine Press, with its Dolphin-and-Anchor that was to become a symbol of printing, was founded in Venice by Aldus Manutius using fonts that were exact counterfeits of the best existing forms of hand-lettering employed by scribes of the age. Early publications naturally concentrated on the classics and, in 1495, Aldus began the production of the works of Aristotle, the fourth volume subsequently becoming so rare that four years later Erasmus complained in a letter that he had been unable to obtain a copy. In that year, Aldus produced *Hypnerotomachia Poliphili*, commonly known as the *Dream of Polyphilus*, considered by some to be one of the finest woodcut books ever produced. The author was an unknown Dominican monk, Francesca Colonna, but the 170 illustrations are believed to be the work of Bellini, although it has also been suggested that the artist was Raphael. At an auction in 1977 a first edition, bound in modern vellum boards, fetched £7,800.

But the big breakthrough was Aldus' introduction of the italic font, said to be based on the thin, inclined handwriting of Petrarch. The first full application of this typestyle was in his *Vergilivs* (Virgil—1501), although he had used it for effect in a few odd words the year before. This minor revolution resulted in a rush of work, which not only enabled him to employ a hand-picked band of printers but also created a boom in forged works using the by now distinguished name of Aldus. In later years forty or fifty titles, forged in his name, were discovered as far away as Basle and Lyons. When Aldus died the firm continued to produce fine books, although gradually the standard deteriorated, it being suggested that Aldus Manutius the Younger was more interested in writing than in the craft of printing. However, many interesting titles emerged from the press in the early years after his death, such as *Lvciani: Dialogi et Alia Mylta Opera* (1522). In referring to this book in his bibliography, *Bibliothica Curiosa* (revised and corrected Edmund Goldsmid, 1887), Renouard says: '. . . care should be taken to see if pages 385–392 and 435–440 have not been torn out, as they were suppressed by the Inquisition.'

Venice produced more than half of the books published in Italy during the first hundred years of printing, and another local printer, whose operation was later to be combined with that of Aldus, was the Frenchman Nicolas Jenson (1420–80), who is credited with designing the roman face that inspired William Morris' 'Golden' type and the Doves Press style. The story goes that in 1458 Jenson was sent by the King of France to Mainz to discover Gutenberg's secret. Whatever he discovered, Jenson did not return to France but made his way to Venice. A man of unquestioned talent, he has been the subject of enormous speculation, portrayed as a flamboyant extrovert to the degree of conceit; but there seems little evidence to substantiate this assertion. For example, manuscripts and early printed books had no title page (one speculates that this was because of the high cost of paper), and a book would open simply with 'Here beginneth', followed by the name of the author and the subject; and, at the end, were the printer's name and the date. Occasionally the printer would add a little comment, or even a discreet commercial, but in the main he chose to maintain a low profile. Critics of Jenson have used the following eulogy as an example of the man's conceit:

> This edition [of *De Veritate Catholicae Fidei*] was furnished us to print in Venice by Nicolas Jenson of France . . . Kind towards all, beneficent, generous, truthful and steadfast in the beauty, dignity and accuracy of his printing, let me—with the indulgence of all—name him the first in the whole world; first likewise in his marvellous speed. He exists in this, our time, as a special gift from Heaven to men. June thirteen, in the year of Redemption 1489. Farewell.

But, since Jenson had been dead for nine years, I think he can be exonerated from blame.

Before leaving the question of title pages, one should mention that most authorities believe that the man who started them—not necessarily the first man to splash out with his paper ration—was the German printer Ther Hoernen of Cologne, in 1470. By the end of the century they had come to stay, and printers were showing great ingenuity in arranging type in the form of wine cups, funnels, inverted cones and half diamonds. And, in the same way that, centuries earlier, the monk-scribes had turned simple transcriptions into ornate works of art, so in the sixteenth century artists such as Dürer, Holbein, Rubens and Mantegna executed engraved titles so beautiful that they looked incongruous against the generally poor typography. Inevitably, as the art of printing declined, so did that of the engraved title, but that was some time later.

Two names we all recognise are those of Gutenberg and Caxton. The former, Johann Gutenberg (1397–1468) of Mainz, famous for his invention of movable type (although this is disputed) and for his printing of the world's most valuable book: the Bible that bears his name, the forty-two-line version of 1452–5 and thirty-six-line edition of 1457–9. Only forty-eight Gutenberg bibles of the less than two hundred originally printed—about a hundred and fifty on parchment and forty on vellum—are known to exist, over twenty of which are imperfect, so that the rarity factor is the main feature in today's market value. But the book is a work of art by any standards. The illuminations are beautiful, although not outstandingly so considering the incredible standards maintained in this type of work; but the preservation of the print makes its origins from a primitive hand-press almost unbelievable. The evenness of print and ink, the accurate alignment of the letters and the sharpness of impression are equal to anything achieved by the modern presses. Printing the Bible was one thing, but imagine the headache of trying to collate, from six hand-presses, 641 pages of double-columned type—with no page numbers or any obvious sequence mark? With the value of a good copy of the original set at well over one million pounds, it is ironical that poor Gutenberg thought he had a flop on his hands.

The Bible was financed by a loan of eight-hundred Guilders, which in 1450 was equivalent of the cost of ten townhouses or three or four country estates. In the process of producing the Bible Gutenberg conceded half his business. But, even without unions with which to contend, he found production costs shooting up and had to borrow the same amount again. This time his moneylender partner, a shrewd lawyer called Johannes Fust, foreclosed—taking the completed Bibles and the printing works. But, since Fust had acquired an appetite for printing, he put the printing works to good use, forming a partnership with a printer called Schoeffer, and in 1457 their names appeared on the famous *Psalter*, the first time a firm of printers had included their mark.

William Caxton (1422–91) means a lot to the English-speaking peoples. He may not have been a genius but he was the best we had, and the first in a slow building but healthy printing industry in England—where from 1476, when he started, to 1600, there are records of 350 printers, and nearly 10,000 separate titles, although many were of single sheets. It is thought that Caxton learned about printing in Cologne, although he printed his first book at Bruges between 1474 and 1475, before returning to England, setting up at Westminster. In 1477, the first book printed in England, *The Dictes or Sayengis of The Phylosophers*, came off his presses at Westminster, although it was such a novelty that few copies ever reached the booksellers of the day. A year later he published the *editio princeps* (term for the first printed version of a manuscript) of *The Canterbury Tales*, later printing a second edition.

In fact, many of the tributes paid to Caxton are more for his service to the English language than for his work as a printer. He reproduced not only the classics but his own translations from French legend and romance. He might, for example, be credited with the deep-rooted establishment of the King Arthur legend, since he put into print, and so into the hands of thousands who would not otherwise have seen it, Malory's *Morte d'Arthur*, which had sown the seed. (It seems strange, incidentally, that Malory's inspired translation of such a wonderful story should not have been re-examined and revised until John Steinbeck tried to tackle it centuries later, with his incomplete version being published after his death.)

Men like Elzevir, Bodini, Didot and Baskerville all made their mark on the development of the printed page, but I confess that my attitude to print has much in common with the enthusiastic amateur who qualifies his interest in, say, music and art by declaring: 'I know what I like.' Most of us know what we like, and the contribution of individuals who may have preferred one font shape to another, or crossed one with another to produce a 'hybrid', is of little interest except to the student of typography. Accordingly, let us jump a few hundred years, with only a brief reference to two interesting areas, illustration and private presses. As I have stated, illuminated manuscripts were more works of art than of literature, and the advent of printing proved no handicap to artists. Incredibly, colour was introduced to the handpresses in Germany as early as 1457, with the use of red and blue in capital letters. Certain subjects lent themselves to illustration and *The Book of Hours*, for example, continued to attract printers and their artists. In 1508 the French illustrator Jean Bourdichon was paid 1,050 *livres tournois* for decorating 238 vellum leaves in the

Book of Hours of Anne of Brittanny (wife of Louis XII); or, as the period equivalent of a remittance advice said, for 'richly and sumptuously historiating and illuminating a great Book of Hours for our use'.

Private presses are worth a mention at this stage simply because many people assume that they are an innovation of the nineteenth and twentieth centuries. In fact the first British imprint was probably the Strawberry Hill Press, started in 1757 by Horace Walpole, which, within a year produced *Odes of Thomas Gray* (Gray was a patron of Walpole). Inevitably the idea has attracted (and still does) a number of amateur enthusiasts, some good and some less than indifferent. One, Middle Hill Press, was started by Sir Thomas Phillips, the bibliomaniac to whom I have already often referred; while he had the will, the craftsmen he employed were not what they might have been. But some presses were good, very good, and it was what one might call the first of the modern private presses, William Morris' Kelmscott Press, that in 1891 shook the printing world from its lethargy and set new standards.

The Kelmscott edition of Chaucer epitomises the peaks sought and achieved by Morris. The publication date of 1896 rather dismisses the incredible effort and talent poured into the book— which took nearly five years to prepare, three and a half years to execute, and twenty-one months to print. Limited to 425 copies, with forty-six bound by T. J. Cobden-Sanderson at the Doves Bindery, it is hardly surprising that good copies today would fetch well over £5,000. Consider the following: eighty-seven illustrations by Edward Burne-Jones; one full-page woodcut title (the book size was 15in × 10¼in); fourteen large borders; eighteen frames for pictures; twenty-six large initial words, all designed by Morris; plus smaller initials and designs for binding in white pigskin, with silver clasps, executed by Douglas Cockerell. And that was just the decoration! The special talent of Morris lay in a page of type that was not only easily readable (after all, a book is meant to be read, not just admired) but also aesthetically satisfying. A fan of his, George Bernard Shaw, said in a letter to the American printer William Dana Orcut:

99% of the secret of good printing is not to have patches of
white, or trickling rivers of it trailing down a page, like rain-
drops on a window. Horrible! *White* is the enemy of the printer.
Black, rich fat, even black, without grey patches, is, or should
be, his pride. Leads and quads and displays of different kinds
of type should be reserved for insurance prospectuses and
advertisements of lost dogs.

Nor was there evidently room for grey in George Bernard Shaw's
point of view!

Cobden-Sanderson (1841–1922) realised the principles laid
down by Morris more consistently than his friend and mentor,
and many consider him to be the superior craftsman. Actually the
Doves Press style is very simple compared with the ornateness of
Morris. 'I always give greater attention in the typography of a
book, to what I leave out than to what I put in,' he said. A fascinating man, in talent and personality (he was reckoned to be so
absentminded that, while he would remember to keep appoint-
ments, it was seldom on the right day), there is something of a
tug-of-war today between printers and binders over where his
main interests lay. His Doves type was hailed as one of the most
graceful typefaces in existence, while the work done at the Doves
Bindery has earned him the title of 'father' of the modern school
of binding.

It took Cobden-Sanderson a long time to find his true forté as a
craftsman. At seventeen he was apprenticed as an engineer, but he
decided he did not like business and read for Cambridge with the
intention of entering the Church. But, at Trinity College, he
studied mathematics for three years, opting out at the last moment
before taking his degree (which he would have got) because he
objected to the competitive system. For seven or eight years he
devoted himself to the study of Carlyle and of literature, concentrating on German philosophy. At the beginning of the
1880s he was finishing an exhausting several-year stint revising
the by-laws of a railway, and looked round desperately for a
complete contrast. It was William Morris' wife who encouraged
him to take up bookbinding. The Doves Bindery, opened in
1881, started a tradition of semi-amateur, but more innovative,

binding which ended in the formation of a Guild, which itself evolved into what is today known as the Designer Bookbinders.

What do we mean today by 'fine binding'? Well, on the one hand
there are the masterpieces so beautiful to contemplate that one is
reluctant to open them; on the other, volumes best described by
George Murray of J. N. Bartfield: 'It's like having children and
never being able to hug them. Fine bindings are so beautifully
constructed and durable that handling them is a joy. They are
alive, and warm and pleasurable, in themselves.' The sort of book
he describes so vividly looks much the same after a couple of
hundred years; and, if you are lucky enough to find something
that pleases you from the nineteenth century, the chances are
that it will almost certainly be cheaper than having the same book
rebound today—with, perhaps, not quite the same finish.

It all started with what was called the Byzantine school of
binding from the sixth century when monks bound manuscripts
between thick boards, which they then decorated with metal and
jewels. But since there were a lot of philistines around, more
interested in the jewels than the binding or contents and who
resorted to digging into the wood in search of them, not many
survived. Nevertheless, by the eleventh and twelfth centuries,
with ideas gathered from Europe, British monks began to corner
the market, introducing the concept of leather stretched over the
boards. With the new challenge of print the jobs became separated,
and binding developed in different ways. Gold leaf became
available and, by the start of the sixteenth century, outstanding
examples of contemporary design were being produced. Morocco
leather was being used now, and, with the aid of fine, delicate
tools for impressing designs on covers, new vistas were opened
up. One of the foremost artists in this new sphere was Jean
Grolier, a Frenchman who had been treasurer to the Duchy of
Milan. He inspired a French school of binders that remained at
the top of the tree until the end of the eighteenth century, although
there were brilliant individuals working in several European
countries, including Italy, England, and Germany, where the
preference was for books bound in pigskin, vellum or calf. Many

people believe, however, that the French have never lost that head-start Grolier gave them.

Approaching modern times, the craft was revitalised by Morris and Cobden-Sanderson, and fine binding stayed in a healthy state through the second half of the nineteenth century, during which large British firms like Rivière, Zaehnsdorf, and Bedford (which closed in 1890) were each employing up to one hundred skilled craftsmen. They were to some extent capitalising on a fashion which had begun well before the advent of the 'modern' hardback (the cloth-bound book) in the nineteenth century and which retained its momentum until well after—taking one's paper-bound acquisition to one's 'personal' binder, in the same way as one went to the tailor and the picture framer. The boom lasted until the outbreak of World War I, when it started to become fashionable to collect books in their original state. Today, the only really large old-style binders—although small by comparison with the giants of the past—are George Bayntun of Bath, UK (which incorporates Rivière), and Sangorski and Sutcliffe of London, both of which have the ability to match and reproduce old bindings, bringing work from all over the world. But the biggest binder in the world is not a commercial undertaking; it is the British Museum.

So now there are virtually two schools of binding: the traditional craftsmen, who process about ninety per cent of the industry's requirement, through mainly routine and repair work; and the modern, creative binder who produces the special 'one-off' covers for collectors and museums. It is the former who have to contend with such criticisms as 'fine binding is dead' when they are not only untrue but unfair. Circumstances have changed, and there are only a fraction of the number of craftsmen available, but it is still possible to have books beautifully bound—if you can afford it. The gradual disappearance of the craftsman affects society as a whole, and not just individual trades; it has been suggested that the mass unemployment of the late 1970s might encourage a mini-renaissance. However, with society's present sense of values, it is difficult to see the situation changing radically.

Apart from the shortage of skilled workers, costs have escalated to the extent that it is more economical to buy old sets of books than new ones. There is an old book-trade joke about customers who complain at the price of rare first editions when they can get a new copy of the same title at the local bookshop for a fifth of the price. In binding, the reverse is true. Beautiful sets such as those churned out throughout the second half of the nineteenth century and virtually 'dead' by 1930—and not so long ago regarded as 'furniture' to be purchased by the yard for decoration—can still be acquired for about three pounds a volume, whereas to reproduce the same volume today would cost about fifteen pounds. Even exceptionally beautiful antiquarian sets become relatively cheap in the light of modern prices, although it is impossible to reproduce them. One of the finest I have examined was in the possession of J. N. Bartfield who, of course, specialises in this area: it was a fifty-one(large)-volume collection of Sir Walter Scott's Waverley Novels, limited to twelve sets, with extra illustrations (that is, extra plates added after printing). The binding was of autumn-leaf-calf with goldleaf armorial plate (Sir Walter's own coat of arms, I believe) and thistle corner pieces, backs gilt with thistles; wide inner dentelles (border) extended from the cover, with doublures (inside covers) faced with cream levant also bearing the gilt coat of arms, gilt edges, and red moire-satin end papers. The plates were hand coloured. The price was $4,500; that is, about £45 a volume.

In general original sets will not only look as fresh as the day they were first sold but the leathers will have been better treated and prepared. Indeed, it has been suggested that, while the modern craftsman may be competent at the mechanical aspect of the job, he is handicapped by the materials available. I regard this as an exaggeration, since one can still acquire almost any constituent part, providing one is prepared to pay for it. This applies to other aspects of book production. Hand-made paper, for example, may be highly desirable but costs are astronomical, and there are several papers which look practically the same, so inevitably one compromises. One knows from experience that a good morocco binding can look as handsome two or three hundred years after leaving the bindery, but whether one carefully produced today will last the course depends on other considerations such as one's lifestyle. For example, one thing that makes a leather binding, especially calf, suffer is the high temperature and low humidity of central heating.

This section of the trade, although leaner than fifty years earlier, was nevertheless ticking over satisfactorily until two setbacks occurred in tandem in the mid 1970s. The first was a minor recession (in the USA particularly), when many large bookstores closed their antiquarian departments as specialist staff of a certain generation reached retiring age; this considerably reduced the market. Normally, when sales potential is cut, one compensates by reducing overheads, but the opposite happened in the UK, when the major wage increases of 1974 and 1975 sent production costs rocketing. Today, the established bindery, which does not have to contend with the considerable outlay on tooling, estimates that costs are broken down into: labour 70 per cent, materials 18 per cent and overheads 12 per cent. This means that the average cheaper binding (made with three-quarters leather) cannot cost much less than twenty pounds, or fifteen pounds for each volume in a set. One can probably get more attractive prices from the one-man operation, but he is usually handicapped by the number of traditional tools (required for the patterning like the *fleur de Lys* bracelet he owns. At one European bindery I saw a job for an overseas firm who had complained to me that they had been disappointed by the standards maintained at that bindery, and would not use it again; before long they needed to rebind Volume Two of a work and to match it to Volume One, and presumably there was no other bindery which could do that matching.

Talking of tooling, possibly the world's largest collection of bookbinding implements, which incorporates nearly 11,000 brass engraved tools for impressing designs on backstrips, engraved brass blocks for larger designs on front and back covers, and elaborate or simple line designs on wheels to roll borders and edges, can be seen at a Museum of Bookbinding, opened in Bath in 1977. The museum is an annexe to the binders and booksellers George Bayntun, founded in 1894 by a Bayntun who began in a fairly casual way by binding books and magazines for private and trade customers. With the incentives of higher profits and of buying and

selling recovered or restored works, he began to employ specialists from London to raise the standards of craftsmanship. Establishing a reputation for good work at low prices, he employed his
profits by reinvesting in the acquisition of several small binderies
on the retirement of their owners. He moved into the major
league when he bought the Robert Rivière firm, famous Regency
bookbinders, in 1939. With it went a huge collection of tools and
plant which forms the nucleus of the museum's display, including
not only historic presses but type and larger hand letters in many
faces. Some of the patterns follow the style of famous artists and
illustrators of the eighteenth and nineteenth centuries, although
relatively few are actually used these days.

Since the museum endeavours to cover the history of the craft
from Roman times, much of the display concerns technical
innovation in book construction. We tend to forget, for example,
that binderies are equally concerned with the restoration of books,
and not just with covers. Foxing, for example, that irritating rash
of brown spots affecting ageing paper, can be treated by a
bleaching process, the whole area then being stained to match the
rest of the paper. Most old books in for rebinding have an automatic 'wash and brush-up' as well as a trim before getting
decked out in their new finery. So, while there is an abundance of
technical information and examples of various styles of binding,
including vellum, leather, cloth, velvet, embroidered, silver-
mounted and so on, as well as highlights such as the complete set
of ten covers of *The Anglo-Saxon Review*, edited by Lady Randolph
Churchill, which were reproductions of important earlier binding, many bibliophiles will also be fascinated by other exhibits.

There is, for example, a small, rather nondescript, book—
The Art of English Poetry by Edward Bysshe, published in 1714—
which in appearance does not merit a second glance. Yet, as
enthusiasts have discovered, often by accident when a binding
disintegrates, ordinary covers can conceal a buried treasure; the
reason is that covers were usually built up with 'scrap' paper, and
what seventeenth- and eighteenth-century binders regarded as
waste you and I might regard as something very special. In this
case it was sheets from *Bartholaeus Anglicus*, quarto, printed in
Westminster, by Wynkyn de Worde in 1495. The 'waste' was

bound sandwich-fashion between the leather and board, and between the board and paste-down.

Another little known craft popular around the 1820s was fore-edge painting, painting fractionally above the edge so that the picture is invisible when the book is closed and is seen only when the leaves are placed at an angle. The exhibit comes from the specialist Edwards bindery at Halifax, although there are several examples in the bookshop part of Bayntuns. Indeed, quite a few antiquarian booksellers have copies lying about in odd corners, although some of those offered these days are really modern 'forgeries'.

Inevitably one encounters exotic bindings, most of which are more valuable than the book's actual contents. I once saw a beautiful binding for *The Romantic Life of Shelley*, by Francis Gribble, outstanding not only for the best leathers and silks worked by fine craftsmen but for a unique watercolour miniature of Shelley set into the cover. Indeed, miniature portraits under glass set into covers were once quite fashionable.

However, painting as opposed to onlay (built-up) illustrations are understandably frowned upon by craftsmen. When I was last at Bayntuns there was an exhibit simply and beautifully demonstrating the art of onlay work carried out by the late Robert Salter, a specialist in the field. The book was a signed and limited edition of Edgar Allan Poe's *The Bells*, which in an ordinary binding might have been worth about £100. The binding was in full cape morocco, with modelled onlays reproducing one of Edmund Dulac's illustrations set in a sunken panel in the front cover surrounded by a gilt interlacing design. The book, not for sale, was valued at £750.

However, one must not assume that lavish and expensive bindings are necessarily beautiful; they can be garish and even bizarre. One such unusual collection came into the possession of Seymour Hacker, of Hacker Books in Manhattan. The books belonged to Maurice Hammoneau, a French antiquary who recased each volume in a binding appropriate to its subject; since most concern animals, wild and domestic, the visual effect of a couple of rows on the bookshelves is riveting. Hammoneau's peculiar

hobby began when he bought a book on the Foreign Legion
called *Greater Love Hath No Man,* by Alice Weekes (Boston, 1939).
Since he had flown in the distinguished Lafayette Escadrille
squadron in World War I and was fascinated by military tradition,
he rebound the book in the dark- and light-blue uniform of a
legionnaire, with gilt buttons on the spine, campaign ribbons
and *fourragères* mounted on the cover. As though to prove it was
tradition, and not patriotic fervour, that had inspired him, he
bound a copy of Erich Maria Rémarque's *All Quiet on the Western
Front* in the rough field-grey cloth uniform and brass buttons of
the German infantryman of that era, less ornate and sombre
enough to match the literary content. Subsequently, Hammoneau
developed a passion for big-game-hunting, and started binding
appropriate titles in skins of the animals and reptiles he killed,
skinned and tanned himself. The list is unusual enough to
reprint:

Ostriches and Ostrich Farming. London, 1879.
8vo bound in ostrich hide with a gilt onlay ostrich decoration,
with special handmade ostrich-decorated silk endpapers.

Pig-Sticking, or Hog-Hunting. London, 1889.
8vo, wild boar hide, pictorial gilt onlay of boar-hunting scene,
specially made silk endleaves.

The Water Buffalo. Saco, Maine, 1922.
4to, buffalo hide, specially made silk endpapers.

Modern Milk Goats. Philadelphia, 1921.
8vo, full morocco, specially made decorated silk endpapers.

The Individuality of the Pig. New York, 1928
8vo, full pigskin.

A Voyage to the Arctic in the Whaler Aurora. Boston 1911.
8vo, Full black sealskin, spine lettering inlaid in white sealskin,
seal portrait onlaid in seal fur on the cover, specially made
decorated silk endpapers, slipcased.

Shark! Shark! New York, 1934.
8vo, full sharkskin, specially made decorated endpapers.

Reptiles of the World. New York, 1933.
8vo, full python, specially made decorated silk endpapers.

The History and Romance of the Horse. New York, 1941.
8vo, full cordovan.

The American Shepherd. New York, 1845.
8vo, full vellum, gilt decorated leather labels, specially made decorated silk endpapers.

The Alligator and its Allies. New York, 1915.
8vo, full alligator, marbled endpapers.

Dragon Lizards of Komodo. New York, 1927.
8vo, full lizard, specially made decorated silk endpapers.

Marsupials. London, no date.
8vo, full kangaroo, gilt decorated, silk endpapers.

Cutaneous diseases. Philadelphia, 1818.
8vo, full human skin.

With a Camera in Tigerland. New York, 1928.
4to, full untanned tiger fur. Specially made decorated silk endpapers.

Lion. New York, 1929.
4to, full untanned lion fur, hand-painted grass-cloth endleaves.

Our Reptiles and Batrachians. London, 1893.
12mo, cloth, ten colour plates

Snakes. London, 1882.
8vo, cloth. Both enclosed in a compartmented book box, of full boa.

Wild African Animals I have Known, by Prince William of Sweden. London, 1923.
4to, full grevy's zebra, untanned, the mane forming the back-strip, specially decorated silk endpapers.

The Seal Islands of Alaska. Washington, 1881.
4to, full seal, silver decorated with silver-tooled ornaments on covers, specially made decorated silk endleaf.

When I last saw Seymour Hacker in 1977, the collection was on offer for $5,000, and he was not terribly concerned about selling them. Most of his rarer antiquarian items are in fact hidden away, and not for sale. This is not a result of coyness on his part, but of a feeling that better books are disappearing from the market, and that immediate financial return is not the sole aim.

Someone who, surprisingly, expressed interest in the animal-skin collection for technical reasons, while being aesthetically opposed to 'gimmicks', is Philip Smith, President of the International Designer Bookbinders, and himself one of the world's outstanding bookbinders. Smith, author of *New Directions in Bookbinding*, who frequently commands £2,000 for one-off work, symbolises the modern artist/craftsman who feels that traditional bookbinding is inhibited, and even restricted, by its tools. His philosophy is that it is dishonest for creative people to blindly copy a book in seventeenth-century style. 'A book and its binding have to be integrated,' he says. 'I need to read a book, try to capture the essence of what the author is trying to convey, and then interpret it in visual form. One has to be fluid in approach, and innovative in craftsmanship.' This means that, over the years, Smith has invented many of his own gadgets, and has in fact even patented a visually satisfying new concept in leather decoration, called Maril. This is made up of leather waste and scraps, mixed with white emulsion, squeezed and air dried and eventually pressed into slabs of rock-like coloured leather, from which one slices off strips with an inbuilt random pattern.

Smith's illustrations are so striking that at first glance one imagines they are paintings, but every tiny feature is achieved by leather inlaid and onlaid with remarkable skill. Among his novel techniques are: the use of palladium and gold, normally very difficult to mix, for the edges and titles; decorative endstrips (holding the sewn binding), coloured differently at either end to blend with the colours used on the covers; and the use of semi-precious stones, such as agate, not in itself unusual, but certainly in the way he applies it.

Obviously, the number of people who can afford to commission one-off bindings is relatively small, and one cannot live off international design awards. One is therefore tempted to ask why Smith and his contemporaries do not churn out dust-wrappers. The answer is basically that there is far less of a challenge in what is a one-dimensional art form, and that they get greater satisfaction from employing their skills as artistic craftsmen and not merely as artists.

Smith himself got into binding by accident. He was at art school in Southport and, unable to obtain solid sketchbooks to his own specification, decided to see if he could 'mess about' in the binding class until he could make what he wanted. However, the lecturer insisted that if he were to join the class he would have to take it seriously. From the beginning, his originality attracted attention and, on the recommendation of a Department of Education inspector, he was invited to study at the London Royal College of Art, where he went enthusiastically in 1951— still intending to switch back to art at the first opportunity. But, before that could happen, he was bitten by the binding bug. When he left the Royal College he taught art to keep his head above water while he started to put down roots as a craftsman binder. After winning the prestigious Thomas Harrison Memorial competition, aimed at students and inexperienced binders (it is now called the Bookbinding Competition), he joined Sidney Cockerell, son of the famous Douglas Cockerell who worked with William Morris and Cobden-Sanderson. In the two years that he spent with the firm, gaining experience, he was commissioned to create a binding for the Duke of Edinburgh, and that publicity helped establish his name.

To illustrate the restlessness of the man, his need to look to new horizons and artistic challenges, one thinks of his 'book walls'. He started in 1968 with the idea of a centre piece for a one-man show with designs that were complete in themselves, yet, set out in tiled pattern, created a landscape effect. It took him two years to design and produce Tolkien's *Lord of the Rings* in twenty-one 'pictures' (symbolically seven sets of three volumes). As an exhibit it was instantly acclaimed, but no one had conceived of such an art form so there was no rush to buy. Smith was on the point of selling the sets individually—visualising seven customers in different parts of the world eventually trying to buy each other out—when the bookdealer Colin Franklin, known for his foresight and originality, decided to buy it with other individual bindings, including one of Vesalius' *De Humani Corporis Fabrica,* a book on anatomy.

Men like Smith, unlike the traditional school, have to charge on a time basis, and the cost of a binding therefore relates to the intricacy of the design. A beautiful binding for *Four Quartets,* by T. S. Eliot, for example, costs £2,000, while Shakespeare's *King Lear* was completed in 1967 for £566—but ten years later resold for £6,000—which, of course, illustrates the investment potential of one-off bindings. Subjects are not necessarily modern, and some of his most successful titles have been *Pilgrim's Progress,* and the version illustrated by Dali of *Alice in Wonderland.*

In 1977 he was working on Cobden-Sanderson's *Doves Bible* (1905), generally considered to be the great man's masterpiece. The five volumes are printed throughout in one size of the beautiful Emery Walker type-face, with no leads between the lines and no paragraphs—the divisions being indicated by heavy paragraph marks (to me the only flaw in an otherwise lovely page). The only decorative feature consists of graceful initial letters at the beginning of each new book. It is this very simplicity of style, its main virtue, that the owner wanted Smith to match in a contrasting binding, vivid but harmonious with the content. Smith settled for a landscape depicting the Creation in five separate patterns, each representing, sometimes symbolically, such features as the Garden of Eden, God resting on the seventh day, the Phoenix with the Resurrection, the sun and moon, and so on. His only problem was in trying to find a matching typeface for the covers, since the eccentric Cobden-Sanderson is reported to have thrown the priceless original Doves type into the river in a fit of temper!

However, since Cobden-Sanderson was in many ways the inspiration of Smith and the Designer Bookbinders, perhaps he may be forgiven. The first step was the formation of the Guild of Scribes and Bookbinders, followed in 1955 by the Guild of Contemporary Bookbinders. 1968 saw the launch of the Designer Bookbinders, to create a greater awareness of what can be done, and to enable non-professionals to participate, and this introduced printers, book collectors and anyone else with an interest. Of four hundred members (more than one hundred in the United States) only a third are professional bookbinders, but they include a nucleus of twenty or so outstanding artists whose works are exhibited and valued all over the world.

The danger of relating fine books to the beauty of a binding, or the aesthetic quality of the typeface, is that one gets an unbalanced picture. As bibliophiles, we should be more concerned with the book as an entity, and not as an *objet d'art*. To illustrate how far we can lose our sense of direction, let me recount the story of the person who walked into Hodgson's Saleroom in the mid 1970s with what was described as an item of silver. The silver department, recognising a seventeenth-century example of early miniature silverware considered it might be worth about £200, but as a matter of interest passed it along to the book department. What was passed to them, almost as an afterthought, was the only known copy (not in STC) of a tiny 4½in primer by John Owen, Welsh minister and theological writer of the 1650s, complicated by having a contemporary silver binding. Auctioned as a book it fetched £700.

In the search for quality, what the bibliophile looks for is the publisher who has tried a little harder, and therefore, either because of the price or restricted intellectual horizons, is prepared to sacrifice mass sales. Generally this means the private presses— the worthwhile antiquarian books or pamphlets of tomorrow— and the producers of outstanding facsimiles. The publication may be designed to give immediate literary or philosophic reward, and not be concerned with surviving the wear and tear of hand-to-hand readership, although first editions that do survive intact will appreciate considerably because of the writers featured. Or it may be more concerned with appearances. In the case of the former, a publishing company that springs readily to mind, partly because of its name, is Golgonooza Press, which gets its name from William Blake's divine city of arts and crafts. The object is 'to provide works of poetry and prose which, by their spirit and understanding, foster a rapport between the spiritual criteria of the sacred traditions and the concerns of the practising, contemporary artist'. At the other end of the scale is the Basilisk Press—some might say too commercially efficient to be grouped with the private presses—which does a limited edition of the Kelmscott Chaucer edition for £320, or their own titles such as *Tulips and Tulipiana*, with prints by Rory McEwan and text by Winifred Blunt, for sixty pounds (prints thirty pounds).

In the late 1970s there were about thirty private presses in the UK, mostly owned by enthusiasts who care more for the product and its reader than for profit.

One is hardly surprised to learn that Stanbrook Abbey Press was run by nuns. As with 'old' private presses—Golden Cockerel representing the lavish production and The Poetry Bookshop representing contemporary poetry—most titles appreciate quite considerably in value, although mostly because of the writers they patronise. In later years, Turret Books backed their judgement with Sylvia Plath by publishing *Uncollected Poems* (1965) and today it is already worth over fifty pounds. Keepsake Press is run by my namesake Roy Lewis practically single-handed from his home in Richmond, principally to spread the works of lesser known contemporary writers. His highly regarded publications run from individual poems—consisting of a limited edition single-folded sheet with illustrations opposite the text, glued between card covers, for twenty-five new pence—to literary discoveries relating to established figures, such as uncollected poems and drawings of Mervyn Peake in 1965, and *Unpublished Poems and Drafts*, 1971, by James Elroy Flecker. Another interesting imprint is the Barbarian Press, launched in 1977 by Canadian poet Crispin Elsted, studying in England for a doctorate. With a small income-tax rebate, Elsted and his wife, who had long been collectors of private-press material, started with a Chinese poem written by an artist friend in Vancouver, and translated by Elsted, *14 Changes On A Sāo of Huang Bau-xi*. Limited to one hundred copies, fifteen on hand-made paper, the poem is in fourteen parts, each illustrated by full page Chinese characters.

Another category of publisher motivated by strictly commercial considerations, but needing to work to the highest standards, is the producer of facsimiles—companies such as Idion of Munich, who spent several years on the creation of a spectacularly beautiful Gutenberg Bible, limited to 895 copies, for a little over £2,000 each. Authentication was carried out by the University of Heidelberg, of whose original (one of only ten original copies left in Germany—compared with fourteen in the United States and nine in the UK) the 1978 two-volume edition is an exact copy. Idion also produced a much cheaper facsimile of Adam Smith's momentous *Wealth of Nations*, not requiring the special paper illumination and binding of the Gutenberg, for a 'mere' £200! Of course, the purist will say that facsimiles are neither here nor there, are 'nothing', but there is undoubtedly a market for them.

In 1977, a specialist French printer, Atelier d'Art Philippe Petit of Angers, produced two biographies of Kings René and Henry II (Plantagenet), illustrated by a medieval colour printing process, the stencil, that he has managed to imitate. Among the oldest examples of this process (another invention from China) is a wood-engraving entitled *Le Bois Propat* (1380) discovered in Burgundy, then closely allied to England. The use of colour in this process came later, but there are examples dating from approximately 1430. The method of colouring by stencil, once perfected, remained unchanged, but is increasingly difficult to reproduce because of the way paper is made and because of the chemical content of modern inks. The stages include: the visual selection of the colours based on the artist's original; the choice of tint by selecting gouache or water-colour according to the type of finish required; the cutting of the stencil, a thin sheet of zinc, with a very fine point in order to give definition to the area receiving the colour; and the progressive addition of the tints leading to the final results. The process requires exceptional artistry and dexterity since not only must the colouring be just right—inks must not be allowed to lighten or darken, or get smudged—but the operation must be done at a speed that makes it economically worthwhile. As it is, the books printed on hand-made paper were sold at approximately £250, the price varying with the style of binding. Given more interesting subjects, the demand for this type of illustrated book could be considerable.

The emphasis in this chapter has so far been on fine books, but mention of medieval craftsmanship brings us sharply back to earth, to deal with the other half of the 'fine and rare'. Some of the world's rarest books are preserved in libraries and museums, and we trust they will never be sold. Certain items, in terms of historical significance, are practically priceless. The Westminster Abbey Library, for example, houses the great Missal of Abbot Litlyngton, written and illuminated between 1383 and 1384. At the time of the Dissolution of the Monasteries in 1540, when high-church theological works were destroyed (although, in this case, the library also lost all its books printed locally by William Caxton), the emissary of Henry VIII threw up his hands in horror at the Missal, which was being used as a service book. The Dean saved it from destruction by claiming it was 'royal' property used for the coronation service and therefore untouchable.

Although the library and muniment room at the Abbey is regarded more as a source of reference than as a storehouse of historical treasures it undoubtedly has a huge wealth of material within its walls. Two such items are the thirteenth-century Bestiary, full of pictures of birds and beasts, which formerly belonged to the Franciscan convent at York, and the *Liber Regalis*, or Coronation Book (*c.* 1380–90), which was used at every coronation, and has been the source from which all subsequent coronation services have been drawn. Since the library is little known, many readers will be interested in a brief outline history.

At the Dissolution of the Monasteries, the great library collected by the monks was scattered, and scarcely any books or manuscripts survived. However, there were soon attempts to reconstitute it, and the records show that in 1575 Thomas Fowler, the Abbey architect, was engaged in fitting up 'a newe Liberarye' in 'the tower in the Cloyster'. A lease of the house of 1606 refers to part of it being 'some tyme ymployed for a library'. William Camden (1551–1623), the historian and antiquary, in whose honour the Camden Society was founded, was in those early days Second Master at Westminster School and, as a means of earning extra cash, he agreed to 'have a care to kepe cleane, order and dispose, and safelie preserve' the books of the Abbey Library —for twenty shillings a year. From 1591, the library was assigned its present setting, hitherto used as a dormitory by the monks because of its proximity to the adjoining chapel.

The Library's greatest benefactor was John Williams, Dean of Westminster and Bishop of Lincoln, and later Archbishop of York and Lord Keeper of the Great Seal. Between 1623 and 1626 —when he was also building and furnishing at his own cost the Library of St John's College, Cambridge—Williams supplied it with books, furniture and fittings—according to a Chapter minute 'replenish with bookes to the value of Two thousand pounds at his owne propper costs and charges', an enormous amount in those days. Part of the library, including a fine collection of manuscripts, was destroyed by fire in 1695 but, although it survived, the momentum was gradually flagging, and by the time Washington Irving, the writer and historian (regarded by some authorities as the first to give US literature serious standing), visited the Library in 1818 'the door was opened with some difficulty as if seldom used'.

Various librarians made intermittent efforts to restore its former glory, but the momentum had been lost; it was not until 1932, with a gift from the Pilgrim Trust (set up by an American, Edward S. Harkness, for, among other aims, the preservation of ancient buildings and the advancement of science and learning), that it was regained. Today, under the supervision of Howard Nixon, formerly Deputy Keeper of Printed Books at the British Museum, the Library contains about 12,000 books, many of which have considerable bibliographical interest. Among the early publications are Johannes Latteburius' *In Threnos Jeremie*, printed on vellum by Theodoric Rood at Oxford in 1482; a good copy of *Dives and Pauper*, printed by Richard Pynson in 1493; and the first edition of the Bible in Welsh.

The muniment room contains one of the largest and most important collections of medieval and later manuscripts in England. They include:

Royal and other Charters, the earliest being a Charter of King Offa (*c.* 785) granting the Abbey land at Aldenham, Hertfordshire.

Obedientiary Rolls, the yearly account rolls of every officer of the monastery. The finest collection in England, it consists of nearly 6,000 rolls, some of them over 12 feet (3·5m) long.

Manorial Rolls, referring to about one hundred mediaeval manors in various parts of the country.

Chartularies, such as the Westminster Domesday consisting of 685 folios, written at the beginning of the 14th century and containing copies of charters, papal bulls, etc., some of which no longer exist.

The Lease Books, over 26,000 folios in large bound volumes, representing documents sealed from 1486 to 1846.

Treasurers' Accounts, from 1560 to the present day.

Historical Manuscripts, including a roll 164 feet (50m) long containing details of every foreigner living in England in 1543/4, signed by Henry VIII.

I did refer to museums as well as libraries, but one could not begin to deal with the British Museum within the confines of this chapter. It is, in any case, more widely known than most reference libraries, being used by 150,000 scholars in the course of each year who follow in the footsteps of earlier students such as Disraeli, Dickens, Lenin and Marx.

Equally distinguished names have pored over books and manuscripts in the less accessible cloisters of some of our older university libraries. At Cambridge, for example, the availability of what are now rare books goes back 400 years; the records showing that 1574 witnessed a drive to restore the library after the neglect and wilful damage of the Reformation. Among the printed books and manuscripts donated by a committee which included Archbishop Matthew Parker and Sir Nicholas Bacon were the 1571 edition of the Anglo-Saxon Gospels, Caius' *De antiquitate*

Cantabrigiensis academiae, and a copy of the Nuremberg Chronicle. In 1715 George I presented the Library with the collection of John Moore, Bishop of Ely containing over 469 incunabula, among them forty Caxtons.

In contrast, the 'new' Liverpool University, with a history of less than one hundred years, has an impressive collection of rare books built up from donations, money and libraries from such benefactors as Sir Henry Tate, the sugar magnate. Until 1900 there was practically no manuscript or early printed material, so perhaps the most important bequest was that of 2,700 volumes in that year from the library of T. G. Rylands, because it contained 28 mediaeval manuscripts, 77 incunabula, and 83 books printed between 1501 and 1536. Today, the incunabula section numbers 234 items, one of which was printed by Gutenberg's tough partner Fust: Cicero's *De officiis* (Mainz, Fust and Schoeffer, 1465). In a 900-item collection on nicotiniana is the 1604 edition of *A counterblaste to tobacco* by King James I. Another highlight is a manuscript of Gregory IX's *Decretals*, written in 1290 and illuminated in Paris in the fourteenth century.

Many university libraries were bequeathed, or have acquired the impressive collections of famous men. Magdalene College, Cambridge, inherited the library of Samuel Pepys, including of course the original manuscript of his diary, which attracted little attention until the Reverend Smith started to decipher it in 1819. One thousand volumes, part of the collection of Adam Smith, are now in the Edinburgh University Library—which seems unfair to Glasgow, at which he studied and later lectured.

Libraries are not solely the prerogative of centres of learning. Specialist collections are housed at private clubs and sporting establishments, such as the New York Racquet and Tennis club, which has a sporting library of fifteen thousand volumes. Another fascinating private library can be found at the House of Commons, where there are about one hundred and twenty thousand books; in the Victoria Tower there are over two million parliamentary records, including originals of every Act of Parliament since 1497.

There are so many interesting collections of rare books and manuscripts in the UK that, between 1976 and 1977, the Rare

Books Group of the Library Association decided to produce a Directory to include not only the addresses of the more obvious places but also those of societies and institutions, National Trust properties, and even a limited number of private libraries. A directory of that scale and magnitude will take several years to produce.

To conclude this 'fine and rare' assessment of the antiquarian work of art, let me emphasise that it would be wrong to identify these books solely with the wealthy. While it is true to say that beauty lies in the eye of the beholder, and that each of us looks for very different features, there are undoubtedly many books finely produced, particularly from the eighteenth and nineteenth centuries, lying unnoticed on bookshelves, and at bargain prices, all over the country. Often these are the works of 'unknown' writers and poets, and therefore of little immediate interest to most of us. The lesson, surely, is to look beyond the author's name and the title; if time and trouble had gone into the production of that volume, the chances are that the content could provide a pleasant surprise too. Don't just ignore them . . . look inside.

9 Trends

A few years ago I wrote *The Book Browser's Guide* because I was concerned by the imperceptible contraction of the world of antiquarian books, caused primarily by economic pressures. The object was to identify the opportunities to look at and examine books—surely eighty per cent of the bibliophile's pleasure—before buying them. The closing of still more shops, and a corresponding explosion in the numbers of booksellers operating by post, indicates a radical change in the landscape of the book world, not always immediately apparent at close quarters, but certainly evident to visitors from abroad who now have to travel so much further when book hunting.

The antiquarian trade will certainly never die, but the gradual disappearance of the High Street bookshop has had a stultifying effect on the necessary circulation of books because old volumes recovered from the attic no longer have an easily accessible sales outlet; instead, they are more likely to go to well known auction houses. Inevitably, this contributes to a noticeable shift in the balance of power—something which worries many dealers in better books. The more powerful the auction houses, the greater their temptation to diversify into fringe areas and, to a great extent this seems quite legitimate; auction houses might offer free valuations and investment advice, or training schemes for their staff—some of them already do. But the ethics of certain other trends, such as hanging on to unsold books, which become in effect a retail stock, is more debatable.

The training of staff is an issue on which most booksellers are divided. It may not be relevant to the one-man operation, the bookseller who is content to work at his own pace and who does not care what happens after his retirement or death. But, to larger shops, continuity is important. Business might be fine while it remains under the personal direction of an individual or partner of ability; but fortunes can decline very rapidly without a specific inspirational force. Though the number of family businesses is obviously diminishing, the threat hangs over every firm trying to carry on after the death of its founder. Many booksellers are individualistic by nature, and genuinely find it hard to pool resources or operate in tandem; others are simply too autocratic. 'Why should I take the time and trouble to train young Bloggs, when he'll only leave me to start up on his own?' is the most common attitude. And, undoubtedly, it must be very frustrating when that does happen. But gambling on Bloggs is no different to gambling on one's children's desire to join the family business, whatever it is; it could well be that our children intend to follow a life of meditation in Tibet. We have no right to expect anything of young people, but unless we give the talented ones the opportunity to join in, to share, how else can the vulnerable ones survive?

One of the firms with a more enlightened attitude is Bertram Rota of Covent Garden, and it shows in the attitude of its staff. Large booksellers, especially those selling new books, are frequently handicapped by the practical need to employ transient staff, usually students who might or might not care about what they are doing. In an antiquarian bookshop it is essential to have keen and friendly staff. Knowledge can be acquired, but the right attitude of mind cannot, and, the more involved an assistant becomes, the more this will be reflected in his attitude to the customer. Rota's have a staff of between eighteen and twenty; the oldest is in his forties, and five are very young. The selection process for newcomers is carried out with extreme precision, personality being almost as important as aptitude, because of the need to fit into a team.

Once employed, youngsters are given a reading list of books they are expected to work through; they are asked to take ancillary courses, such as bookbinding and restoration (although they will not actually be doing this work); they are taken to auctions; shown useful pointers when books from newly purchased libraries are sorted; given small informal seminars; asked to check facts and information through bibliographies, and so on. And, since every member of the staff is a potential head of department or director, they are given responsibility. If someone can make out a substantial case for starting a new speciality, it may easily be approved by the management. As Anthony Rota points out, the trade needs more 'improvers'. There is no shortage of people at the top and the very bottom, but there is a need for good middle-men or senior assistants, and this is difficult to achieve without adequate training. I can think of a dozen or so important book-shops which will flounder, and probably even die, when the proprietor or senior partner dies, because all that is bequeathed, after between twenty and fifty years in the business, is a reasonably experienced manager who is more a faithful retainer than the keen executive needed to survive the economic climate of the 1980s.

In any case, in the English-speaking countries, we tend to adopt a *laissez faire* attitude to training. Since no qualification is needed, there is nothing to stop a doctor, greengrocer or housewife deciding, if they feel they have the knowledge and aptitude, to open a bookshop with almost no previous experience. It happens all the time, sometimes very successfully.

On the European continent, bookselling usually follows the pattern of a trade or craft. The Germans, for example, with their traditional respect for organisation, not only recognise the need for training but provide it by legislation. Bookshop apprentices come under the benevolent authority of the *Industrie und Handel-skammern*, a sort of Chamber of Commerce with muscle. Appren-tices, protected by law, receive not only decent holidays and pay but at least two mornings off a week to attend lectures at trade and technical colleges, including those set up by the German Book-dealers Association in major cities. Exams at the end of the course enable pupils to qualify as chartered bookdealers, which in some ways has more practical value than an English or American university degree, since in certain sections of the trade—parti-cularly in the field of new books—some publishers will deal only with 'qualified' booksellers. On the antiquarian side life is more flexible, but unquestionably in the German-speaking countries there are far fewer booksellers by 'sudden' inclination than there are this side of the Channel.

Indeed, the whole trade is more clearly defined. There are no strong 'pockets' of activity in country areas, like those we have in South Devon or East Anglia; most dealers on the Continent stick to the major towns and cities. Similarly, there are far fewer auctions, which makes buying more controllable. Although I have concentrated in chapter 7 on the giant salerooms, there are dozens of smaller firms scattered about the UK, where one finds few masterpieces but (at some) a reasonably high standard of 'good' antiquarian and secondhand material. In the German-speaking countries, there are fewer but much larger sales, which take place perhaps twice a year; bottlenecks are avoided by prior consultation and planning. Furthermore, perhaps because of the training already mentioned, standards of cataloguing are much higher, which means that it is not usually so important to make a special pre-auction visit to inspect the lots. Of course, it could be said that, despite the extra time involved, booksellers in the UK and the USA attending country sales often benefit from taking the trouble to go early. I know a number who have picked up bargains which had been inaccurately described in the catalogue, such as rare engravings printed in colour, described merely as hand-coloured plates.

The bookdealer with flair will succeed at any level, and one need be less concerned with giving a youngster the basic grounding than with taking a recognisable talent and moulding it into what is needed in a potential partner. Naturally, given such opportunities, some will still go their own way. But the only chance of achieving some measure of continuity in the business is to help others to help oneself. Meanwhile, irrespective of shops, we know there will always be antiquarian books in circulation. But, at the rate of inflation in book prices, will anyone be able to afford to buy them in fifty or a hundred years' time?

To be realistic, fashions change and prices fluctuate accordingly, so we should determine what we mean by 'expensive'. Yellow

Books, for example, are much in demand principally because of remarkably talented contributors like Aubrey Beardsley. Just after World War II they were relatively cheap, a set of thirteen in mint condition being worth about £6 6s (£6.30)—but we forget that that was then a week's wages for many men. Today, if the national average wage is £50, and the same set is £125, it is fair to assume the price has risen by 150 per cent. But it does not follow that this ratio will increase; indeed it may go down if Beardsley's popularity starts to wane. It must be conceded that the English-speaking bibliophile is very much a creature of sudden rushes of blood to the head, of excessively enthusiastic likes and dislikes. Quite a number of continental booksellers find it hard to accept the exceptionally high prices demanded for the works of illustrators like Rackham, Dulac and Greenaway. What happens if and when we tire of them?

The value of a book depends not only on its age and rarity but also on trends and fashions. For example, will the interest in the pre-Raphaelite period last ten, fifteen or fifty years? Perhaps the interest will, but surely the same astronomic prices will not.

'Documentary' illustrations probably have an unlimited life. Apart from the magnificent Audubon and Gould volumes, frequently bought as 'breakers' for their plates, the biggest upsurge in interest has probably been in nineteenth-century steel engravings, particularly of scenic views. Books like Tombleson's *Views of the Rhine* and *Views of the Thames*, which at one time reached barely ten pounds (and often sold for considerably less), are today fetching over ten times that amount.

'Breakers' are usually copies with damaged spines and covers, providing a convenient excuse for dealers to break them up and sell the individual plates—a practice much despised by most booksellers. To be fair, it really depends on the book we are talking about; there are always a few which it would not be worth repairing. But even these modern wreckers are being threatened by spiralling prices. For example, a Speed Atlas just after World War II would have been worth £120. Today, in good condition, it can fetch £16,000, which means that even a breaker's copy can cost as much as £6,000. Profitability at those prices has become marginal and, if the demand for single atlas plates diminishes, as it probably will, those plates will be worth much more in complete book form.

Perhaps an extreme example of 'fashionable' interests is the rash of books published in the UK in 1977 to coincide with Queen Elizabeth's silver jubilee—appropriately enough there were twenty-five hardbacks, representing print runs of over one million copies and a retail value of about four million pounds—although, inevitably, a considerable proportion were remaindered. However, the chances are that one or two of those titles will be a minor collector's item in fifty to a hundred years' time, in much the same way as the fairly recent revival of interest in Queen Victoria and, to a lesser extent, the Duke of Windsor has put up the value of relevant books. Even so, that interest will last for a limited period.

Similarly, it remains to be seen what place history will reserve for Sir Winston Churchill. Curiosity in statesmen and world leaders blows hot and cold, even among specialist collectors, and one could speculate on the interest in one hundred years' time in, say, John Kennedy as against Richard Nixon. Churchilliana is currently quite fashionable. One of the most impressive of his creative accomplishments was the biography of his ancestor, the *Life* of Marlborough. The four-volume edition, limited to 150 sets, published just before World War II, is particularly noteworthy because it was issued over a period of years, and each new volume was signed and inscribed by the author. But what sets it apart from similar limited editions is Churchill's fluctuating moods over the years, reflected by his relationship with some of the recipients. The inscriptions on succeeding volumes change from the formal to very informal—or the reverse, if someone were out of favour. A one-ownership set with four very different inscriptions is obviously worth keeping as an investment.

On the subject of investment, it may not have occurred to you but, if there were a major swing in the City or on Wall Street towards buying books as part of a commercial investment programme, unrelated to aesthetic considerations, the antiquarian-book world would in effect become a mini stock-market, as with any other commodity. With individuals and organisations buying and selling as they would stocks and shares, what would happen if someone panicked? Or, if someone spread the rumour after a reliable tip-off, that incunabula were 'out'? An apparently wild analogy, on the face of it, but to continue the hypothesis, the offloading of valuable 'property' more suddenly than the traditional book market could withstand would result in a catastrophic drop in values across the board. Admittedly, we are fifty years or so away from that sort of nightmare, but it cannot be dismissed as idle SF speculation, because the wheels have already been set in motion.

The books that will continue to appreciate in value will be those which cannot 'date' or become outmoded. History, as a subject, is a natural. Every country and city has an interest in its roots and development. Sometimes the more 'vertical' the interest, the greater the value. One 'local' history with a reasonable claim to being unique was offered in the catalogue of Scottish bookseller James Mair in 1977. This was a long run, some 1,440 copies of a scarce weekly newspaper, the *Dundee, Perth and Cupar Advertiser*, bound in ten volumes. The paper, now defunct, covers a part of the nineteenth century not well documented, and, although at £750 there were no immediate buyers, Mair was confident that the collection would eventually be recognised for the contribution it makes to Scottish social history.

Personal mementos of the past will always have a tremendous appeal; that is, items such as published and manuscript diaries of the little known person as well as the celebrity. One of the most fascinating manuscripts I have encountered was at an auction— and the writers were unknown. It was a receipt book started by one housewife in the mid-seventeenth century and continued by others, presumably friends or relatives, until the late eighteenth century. The originality of these recipes makes the concoctions devised by their modern counterparts pale to insignificance. Speaking of pallor, the most hair-raising of them reads: 'The bloud of a white hen is said to be a greate secret to take away the freckles of the face.' And, rather more obscure: 'The snaile water good for a Consumption or Janders to cleare the skinn and revive the spiritts.' At the same sale there was a similar eighteenth-century manuscript, covering a much shorter period, but given to more explicit detail, together with the 'authority' for each cure, such as this example (not my spelling and punctuation!): 'This is the famous Dr Sowthen & Cured Mrs Hales (Mr Wyatts Mother) after Her Breast was ordered to be Cut off She had also 2 Issues Cut in Her Back, & in 2 Year the lump which was a big as a large Egg dispersed Gradualy & she lived 30 Years afterwards in perfect Health.'

There is, of course, no substitute for learning and knowing how to check facts, whether with regard to future prices or to current ones. Anything that we know is unique, or even unusual, obviously gives us a head start. I referred earlier to 'missing' title pages, but another area of potential profit is incomplete sets, sets that *should* be incomplete. I once received a catalogue on Canadian non-fiction from the Arcadia Book Store, in Toronto, in which they offered G. Heriot's *The History of Canada* (Vol. I, London 1804). The price of $1,250, for what was a fairly ordinary half-morocco-bound book, obviously indicated something special. Most of us, apart from specialists in Canadiana, on finding it in a bookshop would have given it scarcely a second glance. Its attraction, however, lies in the fact that it is not only the first history of Canada published in the English language but that on Page 616 are the words 'End of The First Volume'; Volume II was never issued. Indeed, a later edition of Volume I merely changed that phrase to 'finis'.

This sort of thing can happen anywhere, and the few who have that extra knowledge can benefit enormously. Fritz Merkel, of the Chantry Bookshop in Dartmouth (Devon), although in his seventies, epitomises the growing number of essentially *European* booksellers why buy material of little interest in one country, knowing that it will fetch higher prices in another. Born and trained in Germany, Merkel did not come to the UK until 1968. He speaks several languages, including Swedish, and anticipated the Common Market before the UK's entry by travelling extensively and establishing good relations with dealers all over the Continent, particularly in Germany where he gained most of his experience in books and in art. In the 1960s, when he was known as Berlin's 'Bicycling Bookdealer', because of his mode of transport, he called at a very exclusive antiquarian bookshop for a cursory search of the shelves, and found a first volume of Karl Marx's *Critique of Political Economy* (1922). He knew that the second volume had never been published, and that what he held in his hand was worth nearly £120. But the price inside the cover was only three Deutschmarks, and he was momentarily transfixed with shock. The manager, misinterpreting his indecision, said: 'I'm afraid that is incomplete—you can have it for two and a half marks.' Next day, Merkel sold it for its real value but, like the true professional, he invested an extra sixty marks in the shop, in anticipation of that profit.

Merkel also drew my attention to the nineteenth-century German historian Theodor Mommsen, Gibbon's German counterpart—whose *History of Rome* (1853–6) was published in Volumes I, II, III and V. Apparently, Mommsen jumped from Volume III to writing about the Soldier Emperors in Volume V and never got round to catching up with the missing years! And, from his English experience, Merkel mentioned *A History of Dartmouth*, by H. Watkin, who wrote and published Volume I, but died before Volume II could be completed.

Although the antiquarian- and new-book trades have little in common, a fascinating 'marriage of interests' took place in 1977, producing a market mix which could induce others to follow. The novelty, introduced by George Braziller of the USA and Chatto & Windus of the United Kingdom, was a paperback series on illuminated manuscripts, quite the reverse of publishing tradition in which hardbacks come first, followed by the paperback only if there is sufficient demand. The subjects, with introductions and commentaries by leading authorities in the various specialist periods, include *Later Antique and Early Christian Book Illumination* and *Carolingian Painting*, and they are illustrated with full-colour reproductions of the historic masterpieces featured. The availability of such material at low prices can only stimulate interest in the originals and in early books in general.

This brings us back to the subject of selling. Shops dealing in new books have the advantage of learning (albeit late in the day) from the highly effective marketing techniques of the super-markets. But the stock of the antiquarian bookshop does not lend itself to modern sales methods. Special offers of the month might sometimes be feasible, but unfortunately valuable cost savers like bulk buying will not. What antiquarian booksellers can do, however, is to get out to meet their future customers, as well as those they already know. This is done in a number of ways, principally through the growing numbers of international and provincial book fairs. In the UK this trend was pioneered by the Provincial Booksellers' Association, and followed by regional branches of the Antiquarian Booksellers' Association and various individual entrepeneurs. It is, of course, true that most of the trading is between dealers but, as the fairs gradually become better known, their public audience is growing. Some people believe that there are too many local fairs, but only the trade as a whole can decide what is useful, and sooner or later this will sort itself out.

There will always be the innovative and energetic dealers, those that get out in other ways; for example, by lecturing to local societies and colleges. But meanwhile much can be done to broaden the appeal of antiquarian books, to actively generate interest instead of waiting for its accidental birth. As times change, and younger people possibly react against tradition, against pomp and circumstance, certain shops might gradually alter their nineteenth-century image. To many beginners, the prospect of advancing through rich, ankle-deep carpet towards a distinguished-looking gentleman, resplendent in morning suit and carnation, flicking imaginary spots of dust off a Nuremberg Chronicle, merely to enquire about the best way of spending one's hard earned pound (or dollar) is a little daunting. There is no need to switch to jeans and a T-shirt, but booksellers could at least aim for a greater measure of informality.

The Antiquarian Booksellers' Association, particularly in view of the attractions of the auction houses, might consider setting up some form of free valuation and information service in perhaps two or three regions. The idea might be met with criticism and controversy but, in terms of education and public relations, the effort would be justified. Of course, it is too easy to put the onus on groups and organisations; the individual can do more.

Could there be something about books that turns the bibliophile into an introvert?

Most other enthusiasts, whether they are propagating religion, politics, or even sport, seem to be fired by a crusading spirit. But the lover of antiquarian books feels he has something in common only with fellow bibliophiles. Crusaders are invariably thoroughly irritating, so forget about soapboxes. I am talking not even about a 'soft sell' but more about a discreet word here and a sharing of excitement there. A public more aware of antiquarian books can only stimulate the trade, and that is all anyone can ask.

Selected Bibliography

Bigmore, E. C., and Wyman, W. H., *Bibliography of Printing*, 2nd ed., 2 vols, New York, 1945

Blanck, Jacob, *Bibliography of American Literature*, 4 vols, New Haven, 1965

Bland, David, *A History of Book Illustration*, 1969

Burden, Eric, *The Craft of Bookbinding*, David & Charles, 1975

Curwen, Henry, *A History of Booksellers*, Chatto & Windus, 1873

D'Israeli, Isaac, *Curiosities of Literature*, 3 vols, 1791

Darton, F. J., *Modern Book Illustration in Great Britain*, 1951

Evans, Charles, *American Bibliography*, 14 vols, Chicago and Worcester

Everitt, Charles P., *Adventures of a Treasure Hunter*, Little, Brown & Co. and Gollancz, 1951–2

Fletcher, W. Y., *English and Foreign Bookbindings*, 2 vols, 1895–6

Franklin, Colin, *The Private Presses*, 1969

Hamilton, Sinclair, *Early American Book Illustrators and Wood Engravers*, New York, 1958

Knight, Charles, *Shadows of the Old Booksellers*, Bell & Daldy, 1865

Lang, Andrew, *Books and Bookmen*, Longmans, 1886

Lewis, Roy Harley, *The Book Browser's Guide*, David & Charles, 1975

Matthews, Brander, *Bookbinding, old and new*, London and New York, 1896

Miller, E. M., *Australian Literature: A Bibliography*, rev. ed. extended to 1950, ed. F. T. Macartney, Sydney, 1956

Orcutt, W. D., *In Quest of the Perfect Book*, Little, Brown and Co. (US) and Murray (UK), 1926

Pollard A. W., and Redgrave, G. R., *A Short-Title Catalogue of Books Printed in England, Scotland and Ireland, and of English Books Printed Abroad 1475–1640*, 1926 and 1977

Pollard, Graham, and Carter, John, *An Enquiry into the Nature of certain 19th century pamphlets*, Constable, 1934

Ray, Gordon, *The Illustrator and the Book in England from 1790–1914*, Oxford University Press, 1977

Rosner, Charles, *The Growth of the Book Jacket*, London and Cambridge (Mass.), 1954

Rostenberg, Leona, and Stern, Madeline B., *Old and Rare: Thirty Years in the Book Business*, 1974

Seymour, F. S., *An English Library*, new enlarged ed., 1963

Smith, Philip, *New Directions in Bookbinding*, Studio Vista, 1976

Staton, F. M., and Tremaine, M., *Bibliography of Canadiana*, 2 vols, Toronto, 1959–65

Stewart, Seumas, *Book Collecting*, David & Charles, 1972

Taylor, A., and Moser, F. J., *The Bibliographic History of Anonyma and Pseudonyma*, University of Chicago Press, 1951

Taylor, D. S., *Thomas Chatterton, The Complete Works. a bicentenary edition*, 2 vols, 1971

Thomas, Alan G., *Great Books and Book Collectors*, 1975

Watson, Gerry, *The Concise Bibliography of English Literature, 1660–1950*, 1958

Weber, Carl, *A Thousand and One Fore-Edge Paintings*, Waterville, (Maine), 1949

Whitehead, John, *This Solemn Mockery*, Arlington Books, 1973

Wing, Donald, *A Short-Title Catalogue 1641–1700*, 4 vols, New York, 1945–55

Index

Adventures of a Treasure Hunter, The, 87
Aldine Press, 156
Aldus, 156
Alice in Wonderland, 22
An Enquiry into the Nature of Certain 19th-century Pamphlets, 115
antiquarian books, definition, 9
Antiquarian Booksellers Association, 10, 19, 37, 54, 96, 99, 105, 191
Arms & Armour, 106, 110
Audubon, J. J., 37–8, 186
Austen, Jane, 144

Ballade of the Unattainable, 111
Barbarian Press, 175
Bartfield, J. N., 14, 20, 42–3, 87, 165
Basilisk Press, 175
Baumgarten, J., 83
Bayntun, G., 164, 166–7
Bibliographical Society, 58
Bits from an Old Bookshop, 26
Blackwells, 29, 59, 80–2, 105
Blake, William, 86, 175
Bligh, Lt W., 88–91
bookbinding, history of, 164–6
bookbinding, museum of, 166–7
Book of Hawking, Hunting & Heraldry, 74
Booth, Richard, 45–6
Bourdichon, J., 160
Boydell, J., 77–8
Boyle, R., 149
Bray, Dr T., 65
Breslauer, M., 34, 140
Brinkman, R., 49
British Library, 73
British Museum, 58, 75, 88, 103, 164, 179

Browning, Robert, 116–7
Bulwer, J., 149
Bunyan, J., 84, 153
Burne-Jones, E., 161
Burns, Robert, 84–5
Byron, Lord G., 71–3, 116, 144

Camden, W., 178
Carroll, Lewis., 22, 34
Carter, J., 115, 119
Catherine the Great, 147–8
Caxton, William, 57, 159–60
Chatterton, T., 114, 122–4
Childe Harold, 72
Christie's, 22, 38, 88, 137, 142, 149–50
Churchill, W., 187
Cobden-Sanderson, T. J., 161–2, 173–4
Cockerell, D., 161, 172
Corbett, J., 124
Comus, 62
Copernicus, N., 153
Cranberry Bookworm, 78
Cummings, A. J., 108

Dante, A., 86
Dauber & Pine, 56
David, Gustave, 30–3
Davies, Rev S. B., 71–3
Dawsons of Pall Mall, 25
Defoe, D., 87, 108
Designer Bookbinders, 52, 163, 174
Diaghilev, S., 147
Douglas, N., 92
Doves Bindery, 161
Doves Press, 162

Early Colour Printing from Chiaroscuro to Aquatint, 51

Eaton, Peter, 11, 45–9
Emerald Isle Books, 18–9
Evelyn, John, 21, 39, 148–50
Everitt, C., 41, 87

Fanny Hill, 86
Feldman, L. D., known as El
    Dieff, 34, 51, 143
Fenemore, P., 80
Fingal, 127
Fisher & Sperr, 85
Fitch, Canon J., 64–71
Fleming, J., 140
fore-edge painting, 168
Franklin, Colin, 49–51, 77, 173
Fust, J., 159

Galloway & Porter, 37, 78, 105
Gamble, J., 18–19
German Bookdealers Association,
    184
Godunov, Boris, 148
Golgonooza Press, 175
Gould, John, 37, 87, 108, 186
Grant Uden, B. G., 142–3
Great Books and Book Collections,
    155
Greenaway, Kate, 153
Greene, Graham, 128
Grolier, J., 163
Gulliver's Travels, 59
Gutenberg Bible, 96, 115, 121, 176
Gutenberg, J., 157–9

Hacker Books, 168–70
Hammond, Frank, 34
Hammoneau, M., 168–9
Hamnet, N., 47
Handel, G. F., 62
Hanka, V., 114

Hay-on-Wye, cottage industry, 45
Henderson, T. E., 26–7
Herrick. R., 154
Heywood. T., 145
Hobhouse, J. C., 72
Hodgson's ,12, 22, 98, 135, 140–1,
    153, 174
Hornby, Charles St John, 139
Howard, R., 146
Howes Bookshop, 13
Hughes, Howard, 113
Hume, David, 11
Hutton, W., 93

*The Illustrator & the Book in
    England from 1790–1914,* 13
Inferno, 86
Ireland, W. H., 121, 125–7
Irving, C., 113
Irving, Washington, 178

Jackson, W., 104
Jenson, W., 157
Johnson, Dr S., 10, 128
Jonson, Ben, 146
Joseph's, 80, 98

Kay, P., 98
Keepsake Press, 175
Kelmscott Chaucer, 79
Kelmscott Press, 161
Kilgariff, R., 13
Kipling, R., 118
Klemm, H., 115
Knight, C., 44
Kroger, P, 12

Lackington, J., 43–5
Lang, A., 27–8, 111
Lawrence, D. H., 91–2
Lawrence, T. E., 108

Lawrence, T. R. G., 142–3
Library Association (Rare Books Group), 99, 181
Lloyd, C., 77

Macpherson, J., 127–8
Maggs, C., 76
Maggs, J., 88, 100
Maggs Brothers, 76, 100
Malone, E., 114, 126
Marie Antoinette, 82
Medici, C. de, 107
Mellon, P., 78
Merkel, F., 189–90
Middle Hill Press, 101
Millington, E., 136
Milton, John, 84, 108–9
Missal of Abbot Litlyngton, 177
Monk Bretton Books, 49
Morgan, J. Pierpoint, 23
Morris, W., 79, 85, 91, 144, 161–2
Murray, G., 42–3, 163
Murray-Hill, P., 47
Mutiny on the Bounty, 88–91

Napoleon, 27, 73, 137–8
Narrative of Baron Munchause, 125
New Directions in Bookbinding, 171
Nixon, Howard, 100, 103, 178
North Carolina, State of, 40–1

Ogden, C. K., 143
Orcut, W. D., 161
Orioli, G., 28–9, 87, 91–2

Paget, H. W., First Marquess of Anglesey, 82–3
Pantzer, K. F., 58
paper, history of, 120–1
parish libraries, 64
Pepys, S., 63, 148

Phillips, Sir T., 23–4, 138–9, 161
Pilgrim Trust, 178
Plesch, A., 140
Pollard, A. W., 58
Pollard, G., 115, 119
Poole-Wilson, N., 76
Powys, J. C., 20
printing, history of, 119, 155–60
profit margins, 16–7
Provincial Booksellers Association, 191

Quaritch, B., 33–6, 91, 132
Quaritch, shop, 21, 25, 31, 76, 131

Raspe, R., 125
Ray, C., 13
Redgrave, G. R., 58
remainders, history of, 39
Robinson Brothers, 25
Robinson Crusoe, 87
Robinson, Jacob, 11
Rosenthal, A., 106
Rostenberg, L., 76
Rota, B., 10, 183–4
Rowley, T., 114, 123
Ruskin, J., 118

Sanders of Oxford, 93
Sangorski & Sutcliffe, 164
Sarum Missal, 101
Sassoon, D. S., 141
Seven Gables Bookshop, 85
Seven Pillars of Wisdom, 109
Shadows of the Old Booksellers, 44
Shakespeare, W., 113, 124–6, 145–6
Shaw, G. B., 48, 161–2
Shelley, P. B., 71–3, 116–7
Sheridan, R. B., 126
Smith, P., 171–3

Smith, S., 92
Smith, W., 93
Snelling, F., 12, 135
Sotheby's, 23, 107, 136–41, 144, 154
Sotheby Parke Bernet, 78, 129, 142
Solemn Mockery, This, 127
Speed Atlas, 186
STC, 57–8
Stern, M. B., 76
Stevens, B. F., 54
Stevens, H. N., 54
Stevens, Henry, 54
Stevens & Brown, 61
Strawberry Hill Press, 161
Swift J., 59–60
Swinburne, R., 116–17

Tenniel, J., 22
This, Solemn Mockery 127
Thomas, A. G., 74, 155
Thomas, Dylan, 11
Thorp, Thomas, 37, 95–6

Thoresby, R, 136
Tombleson, 186
Traylen, Charles, 14, 36–41, 56, 108, 149
Trelawny, J. E., 116
Turret Books, 175

Venice, its influence, 156
Victorian Age, The, 13

Waller, E., 146
Walpole, Horace, 123, 161
Weinreb, B., 47
Wellcome, Sir H., 25
Westminster Abbey Library, 177–9
Williamson, R. M., 26
Wing, Donald, 58
Wingate, Orde, 48
Wise, Thomas, 115–19
Worde, W. de, 74–5, 167
Wordsworth, W., 85, 122

Zaehnsdorf, 115, 164